Presented To:

From:

Date:

the LOST ART *of* PURE WORSHIP

DESTINY IMAGE BOOKS
BY JAMES W. GOLL

The Seer

Adventures in the Prophetic

Prayer Storm

God Encounters

the LOST ART of PURE WORSHIP

JAMES W. GOLL
AND CHRIS DuPRÉ

with contributions from
JEFF DEYO, SEAN FEUCHT, JULIE MEYER,
AND RACHEL GOLL TUCKER

DESTINY IMAGE₀ PUBLISHERS, INC.

P.O. Box 310, Shippensburg, PA 17257-0310

"Promoting Inspired Lives."

This book and all other Destiny Image, Revival Press, MercyPlace, Fresh Bread, Destiny Image Fiction, and Treasure House books are available at Christian bookstores and distributors worldwide.

For a U.S. bookstore nearest you, call **1-800-722-6774.**

For more information on foreign distributors, call **717-532-3040.**

Reach us on the Internet: **www.destinyimage.com.**

ISBN 13 TP: 978-0-7684-4128-4

ISBN 13 Ebook: 978-0-7684-8833-3

For Worldwide Distribution, Printed in the U.S.A.

1 2 3 4 5 6 7 8 / 16 15 14 13 12

DEDICATION

We would like to dedicate this book to the incredible people who have made up all the many worship teams that have worked with us over the years. You have been more than a team. You have been like family to us. We've always been amazed at your level of excellence and your desire to use your gifts for the glory of God.

This book is a product of your years of love to our Father and your desire to see the lost art of pure worship restored.

So we dedicate this book to worshipers worldwide, and especially to those who have assisted us in our task of helping to lead the way.

James W. Goll, Chris DuPré,
Jeff Deyo, Sean Feucht, Julie Meyer, and Rachel Goll Tucker

ACKNOWLEDGMENTS

*G*rateful thanks to the amazing team of people who made this book a reality. First I want to thank Kathy Deering, who has been a godsend in my life for these past many years and projects. She is one of the most brilliant writer/editors I have ever worked with, and it is always an honor to have her in my corner. You make me and my friends sound good!

I also want to personally thank my publishing friend of years, Don Milam. Together, he and I have dreamed numerous book projects together. This volume is the third in the three-part *Lost Art* series, and Don has been there with me through all of this crazy journey. Don—you are tops, for sure!

I do not want to forget to give thanks to the Lord for Don Nori, Sr., founder of Destiny Image. He believed in me and invested in me when I had no writing experience and I was still in formation. Thank you, Don. You truly are a forerunner!

In addition, I want to thank the new, next generation team at Destiny Image. I am grateful for your dedication, innovation, and desire to publish the "now word" for a hungry world. This particular book has proven to be possibly the hardest publishing task I have ever taken on, but with your help we stuck to the vision, stuck to the Lord, and stuck to each other—and we got it done. Blessings to each and every one on the staff at Destiny Image.

Special thanks go to all of the amazing, talented contributors to this book: Chris DuPré in particular, and also Jeff Deyo, Sean Feucht, Julie Meyer, and Rachel Goll Tucker. Each of you is a shining light in the midst of the people of God, and each of you has brought a unique contribution to the whole. Like King David, you are men and women after God's own heart. Thank you for working with me!

God bless you all,
James W. Goll
(hosting *The Lost Art of Pure Worship*)

GRATITUDE AND ACKNOWLEDGMENTS

FROM CHRIS DUPRÉ

With James, I want to thank some of the wonderful people who have made this book possible. Kathy Deering, you are a joy to work with and I so appreciate all you've done to help pull this thing together. You carry His heart.

Don Nori and Don Milam, thank you for continuing to keep your hearts focused on what God is doing. Your work over the years has changed the lives of countless people. I'm honored to be connected with you.

To my friend James Goll: we have known each other for over 20 years and you continue to amaze me. Your love for His presence is an inspiration, and I know that because as you seek Him, others have found Him also. Thanks for bringing me into this project. It's been a privilege. May we continue to forge out time to enjoy our friendship. Much love.

And last, a big thank you goes out to my wife, Laura. You are a woman of beauty who carries a tender heart of worship. Anything that I do, especially if it is meaningful, always has your fingerprints on it. Thank you for walking with me. I love you.

ENDORSEMENTS

James Goll is filled with an intense, fiery passion for the things of God. His insight into the deeper dimensions of intercession and His presence has been a wellspring of life to the Body of Christ, and he has chronicled this in his book series, *The Lost Art of Intercession* and *The Lost Art of Practicing His Presence*. He now completes this three-book series with one of the most important elements of the believer's relationship with God—worship. In *The Lost Art of Pure Worship*, James sounds the trumpet and gathers men and women who have understanding and experience of pure, true worship to contribute their gems of revelation that will take you into a new dimension of worshiping and loving God as He deserves.

Dr. Ché Ahn
Senior Pastor, HROCK Church, Pasadena, CA
President, Harvest International Ministry
International Chancellor, Wagner Leadership Institute

In today's world there are so many distractions that demand our time and focus, but as Jesus said to Martha, "only one thing really matters" (my paraphrase). Jesus was referring to Mary who was sitting at His feet adoring Him, captured by His love, listening to His every word. In our day, there is still "only one thing that really matters"—complete focus on Him. *The Lost Art of Pure Worship* will call you into the depths of that holy, vital place of devotion and adoration. It is a book that you can read and re-read due to the depth of revelation, insight, and impartation contained within its pages. Embrace the art of pure worship in your life.

Patricia King
Founder of XPministries
XPmedia.com

Living in Music City U.S.A., it has been my desire to see a company of true believers in Jesus arise who live a life of abandoned worship to the Son of God. I am first an ambassador for Christ and I am second a professional blue grass musician and international performer. I thank the Lord for this excellent book that challenges every believer to first be a worshiper of God and then live out their lives in such a manner that their light will shine in a dark places. Become the message contained in the pages of this book!

Ricky Skaggs
Composer, producer, and lover of Jesus
Skaggs Family Records
Hendersonville, Tennessee

A global movement is taking place across the Body of Christ. It is one that restores the proper role of worshiping intercessors and interceding worshipers. It is my joy to commend to you this inspiring book by this intergenerational group of leaders on *The Lost Art of Pure Worship*. It is full of Scripture, testimonies from life, and a purity in its delivery. May you catch the message and live it to the glory of God!

Elizabeth Alves
Increase International
Bestselling author of *Mighty Prayer Warrior* and other books

For over 25 years, by the grace of God, I have dedicated my life to composing and producing music that would represent Jesus well and move the heart of the listener into a deeper place of worship with Him. Behold a book on one of my favorite subjects—Pure Worship—that testifies of the love of God and draws the reader into a more intimate relationship with the One who first loved us. As you read the book, pray that you will embody the message and live a lifestyle of passionate worship to the One alone who is worthy of all praise.

Michael W. Smith
Worshipping composer, producer, and author
Franklin, Tennessee

For years I have struggled with the idea that worship is something that happens when the music begins, or is somehow relegated to the four walls of a building. The great apostle Paul said, "offer your body as a living sacrifice," and yet so many Christians have a dualistic approach to God. They "worship" on Sunday morning, and the rest of the week they work. I have longed for someone to teach the Body of Christ how to integrate worship as a lifestyle, where the only difference between church services and their daily occupation is the type of instruments that are used to give God glory. *The Lost Art of Pure Worship* is a clarion call for believers to return to their God-given mandate to live in a continuous state of communion with God. The authors have done a masterful job of teaching people the lost art of worship. This book could radically alter your walk with God, taking you from the outer court of a boring existence to the holy place of continuous divine encounters. I highly recommend this book.

Kris Vallotton
Co-Founder of Bethel School of Supernatural Ministry
Author of seven books including *The Supernatural Ways of Royalty*
Senior Associate Leader of Bethel Church
Redding, California

A new generation of worshiping warriors is arising. Join in the growing company of Mary of Bethanys who love to pour out their love through worship at the feet of Jesus. May this book be used to encourage and expand the global worship and prayer movement.

Mike Bickle
Director of International House of Prayer
Kansas City, Missouri

Intimacy is everything to me. Being totally united with my Beloved Jesus and participating in His very nature is my highest goal and my greatest desire. As I spend time worshiping Jesus and gazing upon His beauty, I find that there is no other direction to go but deeper in to union with Him. It is out of this place of intimate worship that the fragrance of His love and glory flows to the world around me. Lasting fruit comes from no other place.

James Goll's book, *The Lost Art of Pure Worship,* echoes the longing of God's heart for intimacy with His people. God simply loves being with us and there is nothing that He won't do to draw us closer to Himself. He is longing for the eye-to-eye and heart-to-heart gaze with His Bride. I believe that through this book, the Lord is calling His people to slow down and make time to simply be with Him. We can experience as much of God as we desire, if we take the time to get lost in worship long enough to hear His heartbeat. Our greatest call and privilege is to worship our Savior and enjoy this union of love forever. What a joy!

It is my delight to highly recommend *The Lost Art of Pure Worship*. James Goll is a great friend and an inspiration. I honor all the authors who have contributed to this book, not only as gifted and anointed worship leaders, but also as those whose very lives reflect the true meaning of pure worship.

Heidi Baker, PhD
Founding Director, Iris Global

Contents

INTRODUCTION

JAMES W. GOLL

*T*his book has been waiting in my heart for a long time. It completes the three-book series that began with *The Lost Art of Intercession* and continued with *The Lost Art of Practicing His Presence* (originally titled *Wasted on Jesus*). For this book, *The Lost Art of Pure Worship*, I have enlisted the help of several experienced worship leaders.

Although personally I love to worship in song and in as many other ways as I can, I appreciate the fact that God calls certain men and women into a life of leading others in corporate worship, and I wanted to "share the platform" with them as we explore the topic of pure worship. This will be a much better book with their contributions added to my own.

Three of the chapters are mine. The rest have been written by the others. Chris DuPré shares his heart for worship in three of those chapters. Contributing one chapter each are Julie Meyer, Sean Feucht, Jeff Deyo, and my own daughter, Rachel Goll Tucker.

Each chapter features selected lyrics of hymns and worship songs that declare the glory of God with timeless beauty. In the chapters contributed by worship leaders, the lyrics are their very own, and many of them will be familiar to you. I am not a songwriter myself, but I carry a deep love of the old hymns with which I grew up, and they carry me into God's presence as well as any contemporary song. I have included the words to favorite hymns at the ends of my chapters (as I have been doing in many of my other books).

I once had a Holy-Spirit-inspired dream in which I coauthored a book with my longtime friend Chris DuPré, and the book became part of *The Lost Art* series. At the time, I tucked the idea away, because although I knew that Chris wrote worship songs, I honestly did not know that Chris ached to write books, screenplays, and such. Several of his worship songs are sung around the globe and he has worked alongside Mike Bickle to help establish the International House of Prayer in Kansas City. He has also served as a worship pastor in Toronto, Nashville, and beyond. Now he has a chance to express some of his wisdom and experience in his chapters for this book.

The other specially-selected authors in this book are Kingdom statesmen (and women) in their own right, each with a calling to impact our generation with the sounds of Heaven on earth. Jeff Deyo and I became instant friends after I moved from the Kansas City area to greater Nashville, Tennessee. Jeff, who was the original lead singer for the renowned Christian band, Sonicflood, has written numerous well-known worship songs, and he founded the Pure Worship Institute. Jeff now lives with his wife and sons in the greater Minneapolis area, where he teaches at a Bible college while still touring with his Worship City Band. Sean Feucht, founder of Burn 24-7, is a young apostle of worship and prayer, a singer and songwriter, and an activist who has established over 150 "burn units" across the globe. Now based in Harrisburg, Pennsylvania, Sean is a shining light of the next generation of leaders.

To provide a female perspective, we have Julie Meyer of the International House of Prayer in Kansas City, a psalmist, prophetess, dreamer of amazingly clear dreams, and my "little sis" since my Kansas City days. She is my personal favorite worship leader to this day. Rounding out the team is my youngest daughter, Rachel Goll Tucker. Rachel, a model and budding actress, lives to worship; she sings and composes both secular ballads and worship music with her husband, associate worship pastor Mckendree Tucker IV. They record under a secular band name, "August York."

With this awesomely talented mix of contributors, we have a blending of generations, people with vast experience as well as new voices. These men and women love Jesus and they love the secret place of the Most High. I count them all as my friends (plus a daughter). With them, let's advance a little higher up the holy worship mountain of God.

> *Who may ascend into the hill of the Lord? Or who may stand*
> *in His holy place? He who has clean hands and a pure heart...*
> (Psalm 24:3-4 NKJV).

Let these trusted friends exhort and inspire you to climb the hill of the Lord, worshiping the Lord with clean hands and a pure heart.

Blessings to you!
James W. Goll

Section One

FOR THE
AUDIENCE OF ONE

While he was still speaking, a bright cloud overshadowed them, and behold, a voice out of the cloud said, "This is My beloved Son, with whom I am well-pleased; listen to Him!" When the disciples heard this, they fell face down to the ground and were terrified. And Jesus came to them and touched them and said, "Get up, and do not be afraid." And lifting up their eyes, they saw no one except Jesus Himself alone (Matthew 17:5-8 NASB).

*E*ven good things can be a distraction to the main thing. Even professional instrumentation, great sound systems, and fantastic programs can be nothing more than a distraction to the One who is to have the center stage. A battle is being fought every day. Whom do you worship?

What is pure worship and how do we get there? It comes by pushing aside the many distractions and seeing no one except Jesus Himself, alone.

Chapter One

RESPONDING TO LOVE

CHRIS DUPRÉ

*P*ure worship...Can we have it this side of Heaven? Some may say no, but I say yes. What makes our worship pure is not the surroundings; it is the intent of the heart. Always has been, always will be.

I was saved at 19 years of age. I had just spent a year at college, a very wasted year (in more ways than one), and suddenly I was a new creation—only I did not know what that meant. It was 1973 and my hair, when wet, was halfway down my back. Sounds gross now, but that was the way we wore it back then. One day I was in a room of potheads and the next I was walking into a very loud and vibrant church.

I remember it well; my brother brought me to this little church that he and my sister were attending at the time. It was a Friday night college service. We walked into a room of radical worshipers. A full band was leading people in very upbeat songs. Some were relevant, but some of the songs were very hokey-sounding. The funny thing was, even the hokey, old-fashioned songs had a sweetness about them. There was purity in their worship. It wasn't the music; it was their hearts.

My wife says that when she walked for the first time into a room full of people worshiping, she felt she had just walked into a room full of angels singing. Not too long after that time, she and I got to know a lot of those people, and I can say for sure that they were not angels! What they were, though, was a group of hungry and humble people who wanted simply to tell God how great He is. There was purity in their pursuit of Him.

WHAT IS PURE WORSHIP?

Purity in worship is not the same as attaining perfection in worship. Pure worship is that wonderful moment when a struggling heart is able to get past itself and give honor and praise to the Worthy One, and He receives the incomplete offerings of that weak vessel with open arms. When it is offered in simplicity and sincerity, one small sacrifice of praise becomes something holy and powerful and pure.

How can we create a lifestyle of such praise, becoming a people of praise? It is not difficult, although we try to make it that way.

Shortly after I was saved, I learned that worship is one of the "disciplines" of the Christian faith. Well, I can tell you that I struggled inside when I heard that comment. Up until then, I had been growing in my awareness of worship as a unique, intimate form of communication between my God and me. Suddenly it was to be considered an act of discipline that, like Bible study, is an essential tool in my spiritual growth. That seemed like an insufficient concept, as if Jesus needs to convince the Father to love me because He, the Son, already has. ("Hi, Father. This is My friend, Chris. Would You do Me a favor and be kind to him because he is one of My friends?" "All right, Son. I'll agree to be loving to him, but only because I love You and for some odd reason You seem to like him.") How can we carry on a personal and intimate relationship if we feel obligated to do it in order to grow? That makes the relationship just a means to an end. Something is missing.

I also failed to understand the term, "sacrifice of praise." I put it into the wrong context. To me it meant "a gift that hurts." Worship was a duty, initiated by me solely out of obedience to His mandates. Yes, obedience is a good thing, but imagine a father whose children only come to him in response to his summons, feeling obligated to come. For a father, what a joy it is when your children come on their own because they want to be with you. That is the essence of the heart of pure worship—worship that is initiated by the love of the worshiper.

How many people over the years have approached an earthly king, bowed their knee in reverence, and yet carried hatred in their hearts? I am sure many believers have done that with God. They are in such despair in their life circumstances that if you pressed them they would admit their anger toward God, maybe even their hatred, because of what He is either doing or not doing in their lives. Yet they know they need to worship God. So these people file into church on Sunday, take their places, and go through the motions of their weekly worship service, all the while carrying bitterness in their hearts. Alas, it is all too common.

Please don't misunderstand me. I think that showing up to praise God in spite of feeling bad is an amazing form of obedience and that it can be a sincere expression of love. What is sad, though, is that this becomes the pinnacle of some people's worship experience. Every now and then, when the music is just right and the circumstances of life are just right, worship becomes something different. Unfortunately, it is only every now and then.

RETURNING HIS LOVE

What then can empower us to move forward in life with hearts that love Him as He deserves? I found a key in John's revolutionary statement: *"We love Him because He first loved us"* (1 John 4:19 NKJV). Simple, I know. But it is the key to growing as a lover. To the extent we know we're loved, we have the capacity to then love in return. It is such a wonderful truth. I *can* love God. To do that, the only thing I need more of is a deeper knowledge of His love for me. It might sound a little selfish, except that the fruit of His affection for me is more love for Him.

It's like the old grade-school bar graphs. One bar gets titled "The Knowledge of God's Love for Me." The next bar, titled "My Ability to Love," can be only as long as the first—never longer. I am bound and limited in my capacity to love by how deeply I know His love for me.

This truth and the corresponding process of growth is so important for believers to grasp. Otherwise, we slowly learn how to do this thing called Christianity until, after a few years, we have got it down so well that we have no need of God. We call it Church. But in reality, Church is not a building or a structure; it is His loving Bride. We are His Bride. God has first initiated love toward us, and we respond.

Do you know you are loved? If you do, then you have the capacity to return that love back to Him in pure worship. If you are not sure of God's love for you, then your gift of worship may be mixed with hidden purposes. You may be worshiping to expunge your own guilt. You may be worshiping to try to feel love so you can be sure of it (never realizing that before you ever thought about worshiping Him, He was already loving you perfectly). You may be worshiping because it is a necessary thing, which it is, but if it has become a duty and not a joy, you will have missed the whole concept of relationship-based, pure worship.

God initiated relationship. He made human beings so that He could love us. He walked with Adam in the Garden. Instead of telling Adam to build Him a church or evangelize the monkeys, God just wanted to be with Adam because He loved him. With Adam's sin, what died was not just Adam's body (eventually), it was Adam's relationship with God. The companionable walks came to an end. Habitual duty replaced an eternal relationship of pure love.

SEEING OUR WAY INTO A LIFE OF DEEPER WORSHIP

We now have the capacity to return to that place of authentic relationship with God, because God has revealed Himself to our hearts so that we can really see His true nature and His desires.

Paul prayed repeatedly that people would have this revelation. For the church at Ephesus, he prayed *"that the God of our Lord Jesus Christ, the Father of glory, may give to you the spirit of wisdom and revelation in the knowledge of Him"* (Eph. 1:17 NKJV). Just as eating from the tree of the *knowledge* of good and evil brought down Adam and Eve, the spirit of the revelation of the *knowledge* of Jesus restores relationship. When true knowledge is restored to true believers, true worshipers come forth.

Paul further prayed, asking that *"the eyes of your understanding* [would be] *enlightened"* (Eph. 1:18 NKJV). He was praying for internal vision, internal wisdom, and internal understanding of the true nature of God. We can have our eyes closed and still "see" what we have already seen. The images we carry in our hearts are powerful. Paul understood that. He prayed for our inner eyes, the eyes of our deepest understanding. When those eyes behold something, it changes the way we think, and therefore the way we live.

Initially, our views of God are very limited. We can only worship in response to the image of Him that we carry. But as through revelation our image of Him begins to awaken and arise to new heights, our worship can rise as well. Paul didn't pray only for wisdom or for revelation. He prayed for wisdom and revelation *in the knowledge of Him.* Wisdom and revelation are gifts to the Church so that we can really see Him as He is, and know Him. The more we see of Him and His true nature, the more pure our love and worship will be.

Paul prayed in Ephesians 3:16 that we would be strengthened in our inner man. There it is again. We have this inner self with inner eyes that is waiting for the unveiling of Jesus in His fullness. He goes on to say in verse 17 that we need to be established, or *"rooted and grounded"* (NKJV) in love. We are most intentional concerning the areas of our life that root us and ground us. It is an old saying, but it's true: the root determines the fruit. If you are rooted and grounded in faith, everything comes out of that root system. If you are rooted and grounded in justice, your life bears the fruits associated with that root. Paul is trying to help steer us toward a life spent seeing, and therefore seeking, the beautiful Son of God, so that we can become rooted and grounded in Him. If our goal is anything less than that, we become servants to that goal instead of lovers of Him.

I like to call it, "seeing our way into a life of deeper worship." Again the more we see of His heart for us, the more of our hearts we can give to Him. Something happens inside us when we hear about how someone feels about us. When that Someone is God Himself, praise and worship pour out of our hearts.

HE THINKS GOOD THINGS ABOUT ME

I grew up spending my summers on the St. Lawrence River, fishing, swimming, and water-skiing. When I got married, I began to go to Cape Cod more often, as that is where my wife spent her summer vacations growing up. I fell in love with that, too. The differences were many, but one of them is the incredible sand that outlines the shores of Cape Cod. The St. Lawrence has a jagged river shore with little or no sand, but the Cape has seemingly endless stretches of sand.

It is said that a handful of sand contains about 10,000 grains of sand, and that a milk pail can hold over two billion. That's a lot of grains of sand. I can't imagine what it would take to count the grains of sand on Coast Guard Beach, the beach we go to on Cape Cod. It stretches as far as the eye can see in both directions. And yet we read in the psalm,

> *How precious also are Your thoughts to me, O God! How great is the sum of them! If I should count them, they would be more in number than the sand; when I awake, I am still with You* (Psalm 139:17–18 NKJV).

How can that be? How can such a perfect God look at me like that? On a good day, I can come up with a couple dozen positive things about myself, but the number of good thoughts He directs toward me is unfathomable. Unfathomable and uncountable, but real. Somewhere along the line, I have to just believe Him when He says something that sounds ludicrous to my finite mind.

His good thoughts about me are so numerous that they number more than the grains of sand.

My conclusion, then, is this: I am loved by my Papa God so much, so very, very much, that I cannot fully understand or contain the depths of His love for me. Catching hold of this truth will change me forever. Now I can love, because first I am loved. Worshiping because you see something, or more accurately because you see Someone, is a true and pure experience. Responding to His love—that frames the doorway for the most honest form of worship.

One morning after sharing about God's love for us being the catalyst for our loving Him, a woman approached me to challenge my message. She told me that it was a selfish message and that instead of talking about how much God loves me, I should be talking about loving and serving Him. I asked her if she felt I had said anything unbiblical. She said no. So I asked her where her love for God comes from, and she stood there with a blank face. Then, ever so slowly, a little smile began to creep upon her face. She looked at me and said, with almost a wink in her eye, "I think I understand." She hugged me and turned to walk away, hopefully knowing a little more how deeply she is loved.

Knowing that I am loved—that is the key that opens the door of my heart in so many ways. If I know I am loved, I will be a better husband, a better father, a better friend. When I am secure in His affection, I do not need to draw my life from others because I already have it in Him.

LORD, help me see You & be secure in Your affection...

LOVED IN ORDER TO LOVE

You see, God made you for Himself. He made you so that He could love you. You're not here by chance or by some random evolutionary process. You were made to be loved in order to be a lover. God initiates worship because He initiates love.

God initiates worship B-cuz He initiates love

One of the ways we know we are loved is when our picture makes it onto someone's refrigerator. I am convinced that each one of us is front and center on God's celestial refrigerator. Actually, it's even better than that.

A few years ago I was in England. It happened to be during the celebration of Queen Elizabeth's fiftieth year as queen. Pictures of her as a young woman were plastered everywhere. I watched a video of her being crowned queen 50 years earlier. It was such an elaborate ceremony. When it came to the actual moment of the crowning, the Archbishop of Canterbury placed the crown upon Elizabeth's head. He was the only one who was allowed to crown her queen.

In Isaiah 62 you and I are invited to our own crowning ceremony, a heavenly one. The third verse states, *"You shall also be a crown of glory in the hand of the Lord, and a royal diadem in the hand of your God"* (NKJV). Oh, that sounds nice. I am a crown of glory, and so are you!

Wait a minute; do we really understand that? We are in His hand and *we* are the crown of glory. Now, who is qualified to crown God? Not the angels, and certainly not any human being. Well, who then? Only God can crown God. And this verse says that He has the crown in His hand already. He is ready to crown Himself King. The exciting part is that He has fashioned His crown from His saints. We are the crown that He wears! He calls it a crown of glory, His crown of glory. He beautifies Himself by crowning Himself with *us*. Amazing!

What kind of love does it take to make something so great out of creatures so weak? It is that kind of love we need to understand, because when we do, we fall at His feet, amazed at His beauty and humbled by His glory.

This is the kind of thinking we need to employ when we think of how God leads us through our lives. Sometimes I think we create a kind of backward theology instead. We start out with a false premise that looks something like this: "Life is hard; I am constantly disappointed; I hurt because of what life throws at me—and I know that God is allowing all of this. Therefore, God must be punishing me, testing me, or, come to think of it, probably He is really not all that good after all." In our minds, we create a "reality" about God that is totally upside-down. We fabricate our personal theology of God, basing it on our interpretation of our circumstances and life's disappointing experiences.

Or we use the comparative method of creating a theology of God. "Why, look at so-and-so in the church. They always seem to be blessed beyond measure. They do not appear to carry the type of burden I carry. Why does God not love me as He loves others?"

Either way, instead of seeing God as being good, always, and instead of understanding that He is love and that all good things come from His hands, we use the pain of life as a filter, along with comparing ourselves to others, and we let that determine our personal philosophy about God's nature.

Even the Beautiful People do this. One hundred models, many of whom are on the level of what we would call a supermodel, were asked, "Are you secure or insecure about your body?" I would have expected that something like 75 percent would have said, "insecure," but it turns out that all 100 of these beautiful women responded that they were more insecure than they were secure. Their view had been influenced by handlers who always kept telling them what needed to be improved to make them more beautiful or photogenic. A nip here or a pound there. Their view of themselves came from a fallen culture, not from a loving heavenly Father.

A few years ago, the Lord asked me who I was. It wasn't because He didn't know; it was because He wanted *me* to know. I asked a few of my friends who they thought I was, and I got some very sweet answers. But nothing went to the core of the question. I returned to Him and said, "I've got some nice answers but I want to know who You say that I am."

He answered me in just a few words. He said, "You're a loved son." That answer settled everything in my heart as to who I am. I am His very own son. Therefore, I am loved. As a loved son, I no longer need to find my security or identity from anyone but Him. As a loved son, I can become a better husband, father, or friend because I no longer need to derive my life from those relationships. Instead, I can *give* to those relationships the love and focus they need, because the needs of my own heart are being met by His acceptance and affection. I am a loved son. And so are you—a loved child of God.

We need to recognize how the terminology we use to describe ourselves or our ministries can steer us subtly from a right frame of thinking. When our gifting or our calling becomes our title, it is only a short distance away from having it become our identity. We're sons and daughters long before we're pastors, teachers, or prophets. I am not saying that we should abandon titles. I am just saying we need to be careful that we do not lose our identity as a son or a daughter because it gets overshadowed by our title. I am a son who pastors, teaches, or sometimes has a prophetic word. This may be a subtle distinction, but it is an important one.

Why is it so important? Because if I learn to relate more through what I do (as my title may indicate), after awhile the strength of my relationships starts to be based upon my activities instead of my identity as God's son. Worship is based on relationship, always and forever. Pure worship requires me to know how I am seen by the One I worship, not for what I do, but for how He sees me. Through the knowledge of how I am seen, I respond to that love. It is like any relationship. The more it's not based on works, the more pure it is.

So it is with worship. I love because I am first loved. So simple, so pure.

DANCE WITH ME

(by Chris DuPré, © Integrity Music, used with permission)

Dance with me, O Lover of my soul
To the song of all songs
Romance me, O Lover of my soul
To the song of all songs.
Behold, You have come

Over the hills, upon the mountains,
To me You have run.
My beloved, You've captured my heart.
With You I will go,
For You are my love, You are my fair one.
The winter is past
And the springtime has come.

Chapter Two

THE POWER
OF HIGH PRAISE

JAMES W. GOLL

*B*efore I was ever a preacher, author, or prophetic voice in the nations, I was first a singer and a worshiper. It seems that I was always a "priest to the Lord" first and a "prophet to the people" second.

I started out by singing my heart out as loudly and strongly as I could—to the audience of One—on long walks on the railroad tracks in rural Missouri. Then I sang in the local Methodist church choir (often doing the solos). I sang and sang and sang. I even won singing awards in the high school state music competitions for madrigals, solos, mixed double quartets, and the like. At one point, in my college years, I directed and arranged choral music for an interdenominational singing group called the Seekers, and later I was the lead singer in a trio called the Light of the Day. In the Jesus People movement, I was a part of releasing the new sound that was coming forth.

I bet you didn't know that about me, did you? Singing praises to God was my great love. Honestly, it still is to this day. In fact, one of my next goals is to produce my first worship CD called something like *Inspiration With James W. Goll and Friends*. Never too old to do some new things!

When I was growing up in rural Missouri, my dad wanted me to be a professional singer. Some people even thought I had missed my calling in life. Although I have never made it my primary focus, I have never lost my joy and love of ministering to the Lord, first and foremost, in song. He has always been the passion of my life and He is the one alone who is worthy of a lifetime of praise, thanksgiving, and worship. He is worthy!

FIRST MENTION OF WORSHIP IN SCRIPTURE

It may surprise you to know when the word *worship* is first mentioned in the Bible. Wouldn't you expect it to be used in the context of a story about a temple or priests, or at least in one about psalmists with musical instruments? Far from it. Instead of lyres and priestly garments, the props for the first worship story in the Old Testament consisted of a knife, a bundle of firewood, and a rock for an altar—and the worshipers were two human beings who were absolutely desperate to obey God at any cost. Here's the story:

> *Early the next morning Abraham got up and loaded his donkey. He took with him two of his servants and his son Isaac. When he had cut enough wood for the burnt offering, he set out for the place God had told him about. On the third day Abraham looked up and saw the place in the distance. He said to his servants, "Stay here with the donkey while I and the boy go over there. We will **worship** and then we will come back to you."*
>
> *Abraham took the wood for the burnt offering and placed it on his son Isaac, and he himself carried the fire and the knife. As the two of them went on together, Isaac spoke up and said to his father Abraham, "Father?"*

"Yes, my son?" Abraham replied.

"The fire and wood are here," Isaac said, "but where is the lamb for the burnt offering?"

Abraham answered, "God Himself will provide the lamb for the burnt offering, my son." And the two of them went on together (Genesis 22:3-8).

You know how the story turned out. (If you don't, go get your Bible and read the rest of chapter 22 of the Book of Genesis.) I find it remarkable that what Abraham and Isaac did here was termed an act of *worship*. From our perspective, because we have come to think that worship means singing in the midst of a congregation of believers, the use of the word in this situation just doesn't compute.

Yet when we think about it, we recognize that worship does entail a living sacrifice. Worship—all worship, whether it's in an air-conditioned auditorium or up on a lonely mountain of sacrifice—is an issue of the heart. You can have the best worship band in the Christian world and fail to truly worship if you are not genuinely desperate to lay down your own agenda in favor of His.

✠ ✠✠

THE POWER OF WORSHIP AND THANKSGIVING

As highlighted by the story above, worship involves sacrifice (see also Rom. 12:1), and that means it requires an inner motivation. Abraham obeyed God's command by his own volition. He had a free will, just as you and I do. God's angel did not force him at spear-point to climb Mount Moriah. In the same way, our purest worship arises out of our inner motivation. We do not have to choose to obey or worship God.

By default, we will choose to worship *something*, though. Theologian and Bible teacher Don Williams puts it this way:

Worship money, become a greedy person. Worship sex, become a lustful person. Worship power, become a corrupt person. Worship Jesus, become a Christ-like person. We become like what we worship. But what does it mean to worship? The verb "worship" in Hebrew means to surrender, to fall down in submission—the way we would humble ourselves before a mighty king (Psalm 95:6).[1]

While we may fail to understand it in our headlong pursuit of pleasures, "worship is the spiritual part of our surrender, submission, and attachment to many things."[2] Worship of God involves surrender and submission. This cannot be undertaken lightly, and yet it can bring us great joy. Worship positions us in exactly the right posture—bowing before the One who created us and who sustains our every breath.

We bow before Him not only because He gives us life, although that would be reason enough. We bow our hearts in astonished awe at the revelation of a great and holy God. Worship is the only valid response to God's holiness. For eternity, those who choose to worship Him will gladly worship Him continually, for every act of pure worship on earth bears a resemblance to the worship that goes on everlastingly in Heaven. Here's how the prophet Isaiah described it:

> In the year of King Uzziah's death I saw the Lord sitting on a throne, lofty and exalted, with the train of His robe filling the temple. Seraphim stood above Him, each having six wings: with two he covered his face, and with two he covered his feet, and with two he flew. And one called out to another and said,
>
> "Holy, Holy, Holy, is the Lord of hosts, The whole earth is full of His glory." And the foundations of the thresholds trembled at the voice of him who called out, while the temple was filling with smoke (Isaiah 6:1-4 NASB).

God is in the highest place, exalted above everything else in His creation. It would seem that the only possible response to entering His throne room and finding yourself in the presence of such absolute holiness would be the antiphonal worship portrayed here. What does that sound like? Is it like the rush of many waters? Like a gigantic echo chamber?

Honestly, at least for someone whose feet are still affixed to the earth, another possible response is Isaiah's own agonized cry: "I am unclean! Woe is me!" In the presence of such utter purity and magnificent beauty, Isaiah wanted to perish. (See Isaiah 6:5.) Yet, surrendering his right to himself (after being reassured and cleansed by an angel), he too worshiped.

Even before we get to Heaven or have a vision of the throne room, we can do the same. Matt Redmond writes, "The heart of God loves the offerings of a persevering worshipper. Though overwhelmed by many troubles, they are even more overwhelmed by the beauty of God."[3] In the past few years, I have been overwhelmed with many troubles. I never dreamed that I would go through eight years of an intense fight with cancer. I had never feared it, because it was not in my family line, but it has been very difficult. I never expected that my wife would be hit, too, and that she would have to fight until her last breath. But even in the midst of the heat of the battle, Michal Ann always kept smiling and always kept praising the Lord. She just slipped over to the other side continuing her primary ministry, the one that she had maintained for her 52 years on earth. She continues to praise the Lord!

I still have a lot of questions, but I know what to do with them—I take my questions and I worship Him with my questions. I do it in the middle of the night, on long walks, in hotel rooms, on airplanes. By the grace of God, I have maintained my place of worship. I cannot describe how desperate I am, but also how thankful I am. I love Him because He first loved me and He is worthy of all worship, praise, and thanksgiving. He is my transcendent Lord and yet He is eminently approachable. He loves me, and I love Him. He is my magnificent obsession!

I worship Him, and I am genuinely thankful to Him. I have made thanksgiving the preferred utterance of my mouth, with numerous declarations of God's goodness and my gratitude for it. I thank God for what He has done in the past and for what He is doing right now, believing that He is good all the time and that His mercies endure forever. That is what I have been called to do, and you have, too.

When we lose sight of God's goodness and we forget to thank Him in the midst of difficult times, our mouths begin to leak out the other side; something called grumbling and complaining and criticism comes out, the opposite of thanksgiving. If we don't watch out, we end up surrendering our tongues to the enemy and aligning our cause with the accuser of the brethren.

We can't lose sight of the fact that thanksgiving is just as voluntary as worship is. Whereas worship is nowhere commanded of us in the Bible, thanksgiving is:

> *Let the peace of Christ rule in your hearts, since as members of one body you were called to peace. And be thankful. Let the message of Christ dwell among you richly as you teach and admonish one another with all wisdom through psalms, hymns, and songs from the Spirit, singing to God with gratitude in your hearts. And whatever you do, whether in word or deed, do it all in the name of the Lord Jesus, giving thanks to God the Father through Him* (Colossians 3:15-17).

> *Rejoice always, pray continually, give thanks in all circumstances; for this is God's will for you in Christ Jesus. Do not quench the Spirit* (1 Thessalonians 5:16-19).

Those commands do not imply that we have to believe that our circumstances are fitting exactly with God's will for us. We're just supposed to be thankful. As we worship with words of gratitude, our sacrifice becomes a railroad track of faith and it can carry a payload of prayer:

> *Do not be anxious about anything, but in every situation, by prayer and petition, with thanksgiving, present your requests to God. And the peace of God, which transcends all understanding, will guard your hearts and your minds in Christ Jesus* (Philippians 4:6-7).

Devote yourselves to prayer, keeping alert in it with an attitude of thanksgiving (Colossians 4:2 NASB).

In other words, thanksgiving is the key to releasing God's supernatural power. Even Jesus used this key. Look how He performed the miracle of the multiplication of the bread and fish (see John 6:1-13). First, He picked up the skimpy number of loaves and fishes in both hands. Then, *"having given thanks"* (John 6:11 NASB) and having lifted them up before God, He was able to distribute to the hungry thousands as much bread and fish as they wanted.

Besides opening the way to such blessings, thanksgiving somehow also sets a seal on those blessings. Jesus' encounter with the ten lepers illustrates this principle. (See Luke 17:12-19.) All ten of them were healed, but only one turned back to thank the Healer. And Jesus commended him for doing it. From the emphasis given to that one leper's gratitude, it appears to be as important as the healings themselves.

BIBLICAL REASONS FOR PRAISE

Even without a clear reason, we praise God for who He is. We praise Him because of His incomparable greatness. As the psalmist says, *"Great is the Lord and greatly to be praised"* (Ps. 48:1 NKJV). Although we may not feel like doing it at first, we *can* praise Him in any circumstance. In fact, we can command ourselves to do so: *"Praise the Lord, my soul; all my inmost being, praise His holy name"* (Ps. 103:1). After we get into it, our emotions change to match the reality of Heaven. We offer a sacrifice of praise, and God anoints our hearts with peace, joy, and abundant worship.

Here are seven scriptural facts about our praise for God:

PRAISE IS...

...the place of God's residence, where He is enthroned. (See Psalm 22:3.)

...the way ("gate") into God's presence. (See Psalm 100:4; Isaiah 60:18b.)

...the way to obtain His blessings. (See Psalm 30:11-12; Psalm 16:9; Acts 2:26.)

...a "garment of the spirit" that brings justice and freedom (See Isaiah 61:1-3.)

...a spiritual weapon, a silencer of the devil, and a way to deliverance and victory. (See Psalm 50:23; Jonah 2:1-9; Acts 16:25-26; Psalm 8:2; Psalm 106:47; Colossians 2:15.)

...a sacrifice. (See Jeremiah 33:11; Hebrews 13:15-16.)

...often accompanied by physical expression. (See Psalm 63:3-4; First Timothy 2:8-9; Psalm 141:2; Psalm 149:3; Psalm 150:4.)

Praise sanctifies the atmosphere around the worshiper. Not only that, it clears out the residue of enemy interference. Through praise, individually and corporately, the Church can fulfill the words of Isaiah 52:1-2, shaking off oppression, condemnation, fear, and unbelief; waking up and putting on strength and beauty; being loosed of every burden and bondage, and sitting enthroned, like a queen.

Armed with nothing more than praise, the Church of Jesus Christ obtains a complete victory. *"But thanks be to God, who always leads us in triumph in Christ, and manifests through us the sweet aroma of the knowledge of Him in every place"* (2 Cor. 2:14 NASB).

At the same time, praise is simple. It is childlike. Children do not over-analyze anything. They have a lot of faith, and they take delight in simple pleasures. Even as it reaps a lot of different benefits, praise itself is not complicated. Jesus, quoting Psalm 8:2, said, *"From the lips of children and infants You, Lord, have called forth Your praise"* (Matt. 21:16).

When my faith has been tested, and the enemy is trying to scream in my face, I just toss up a sacrifice of praise. When I feel alone and sometimes abandoned, I just go on a walk and take some time to sing praises to the Lord. It is childlike. It is not complicated. It does not take a doctorate in theology to do this. You just have to lift your chin off your chest, quit looking at yourself and your temporary problems, glance up to Heaven, and give some praise to the One who first loved you.

LET EVERYTHING PRAISE HIM

Not only children praise the Lord. Also, their parents praise the Lord. Aunts and uncles and grandparents praise the Lord. Famous people and "no-names" praise Him. Young and old; everybody praises the Lord God. (This is beginning to sound like a psalm you may have read....) Sunshine and gloom. Day and night. Mountains and valleys. Puppies and crows. Presidents and prime ministers. Fire and hail.... Let's just read through the biblical hymn of praise itself:

> *Praise the Lord! Praise the Lord from the heavens; praise Him in the heights! Praise Him, all His angels; praise Him, all His hosts! Praise Him, sun and moon; praise Him, all stars of light! Praise Him, highest heavens, and the waters that are above the heavens! Let them praise the name of the Lord, for He commanded and*

they were created. He has also established them forever and ever; He has made a decree which will not pass away. Praise the Lord from the earth, sea monsters and all deeps; fire and hail, snow and clouds; stormy wind, fulfilling His word; mountains and all hills; fruit trees and all cedars; beasts and all cattle; creeping things and winged fowl; kings of the earth and all peoples; princes and all judges of the earth; both young men and virgins; old men and children (Psalm 148:1-12 NASB).

By my count, that psalm enumerates 7 things in Heaven and 23 things on earth that are supposed to be praising the Lord—and that list is just meant to be a representative sampling, not a bounded set. All of those things (which is to say, all things) cannot praise the Lord in the same way, but they can all praise Him, and God expects them to do so.

Can anything *not* praise Him? Another psalm tells us that the dead cannot praise God (see Ps. 115:17), but that was written before anybody knew that those who die in Christ will be praising God for eternity. True enough, Psalm 150:6 tells everything that has *breath* to praise the Lord, and that may rule out dead people. But I prefer to interpret those words to mean that the best, most alive, praise comes from the individual worshipers who are directly engaged in some expression of praise and worship. We are enjoined to praise the Lord by any and all means available to us, whether they come to us by accident or by ancient historical precedent (shofar, timbrel, and lyre)—or even by compact disc and digital recordings.

However, I feel strongly that we should not replace do-it-yourself praise with high-tech substitutes. No matter how wonderful the artist or the bands or how pure the sound created in the recording studio, recordings cannot replace the heartfelt praise that streams from a person's innermost being. Yes, they can be tools to encourage you, but the praises coming off that shiny CD do not have breath—until you lend it to them. The high praises of God in *your* mouth, not the mouths of recording artists, will empower you to the max. It may not sound quite as professional as the praise music from recording companies, but there is something irreplaceable about learning to praise God for yourself. You need to exert yourself in some way to praise the Lord, and you need to direct your efforts in His direction.

How can you know how to best praise the Lord? The psalms are rich with visual aids. Psalm 63:4-5 says, *"I will praise You as long as I live, and in Your name I will lift up my hands. I will be fully satisfied as with the richest of foods; with singing lips my mouth will praise You."* Psalm 111 starts out with a picture of congregational worship:

> *Praise the Lord! I will praise the Lord with my whole heart, In the assembly of the upright and in the congregation* (Psalm 111:1 NKJV).

Psalm 47 expresses special exuberance:

> *Oh, clap your hands, all you peoples! Shout to God with the voice of triumph!... God has gone up with a shout, the Lord with the sound of a trumpet. Sing praises to God, sing praises! Sing praises to our King, sing praises! For God is the King of all the earth; sing praises with understanding* (Psalm 47:1, 5-7 NKJV).

With or without other people, we can praise the Lord with raised hands and clapping hands as well as folded hands. We can sing and shout. We can play musical instruments. As long as we are singing *"praises with understanding"* almost any gesture (the glance of an eye, the tapping of a toe, jumping, running) can be part of our worship.

How often should you praise the Lord like this? Is once a week enough, on Sunday morning for an hour or so? You know the answer already. At this very moment, you can be praising Him, even as you are reading this book. You can praise Him every single day (and night), forever and ever, seamlessly into eternity:

Every day I will praise You and extol Your name for ever and ever (Psalm 145:2).

I will bless the Lord at all times; His praise shall continually be in my mouth (Psalm 34:1 NKJV).

Become a full-time worshiper, and you will never regret it.

SEND JUDAH FIRST

Throughout the Old Testament, we see that the Israelites conquered their foes with the ultimate weapon—praise and worship. We know this because of the recorded fact that, of the 12 tribes of Israel, the tribe of Judah was the one that was usually sent first. (See, for example, Numbers 2:9.) The very name *Judah* means "praise" (see Gen. 29:35). The divisions from the tribe of Judah, praising the Most High simply by moving forward together, could shatter the atmosphere of resistance before the warriors from the other 11 tribes even got to the front lines.

In the same way, we need to "send Judah first" into our own situations. Are you facing an intimidating foe? Send Judah (praise) up against it first. Are you not sure you can hold the territory you have conquered? Send Judah first. Do you feel weak and worn out and confused? Send Judah first.

God-directed praise will rally all of the resources of God that any individual or group of individuals might ever need in any situation. Praise is unbeatable, invincible, inexhaustible.

Lift up the banner of praise! Drop your other garments and weapons by the roadside, and move forward like Judah, giving expression to a heart that is filled with godly confidence, awe, and courage. Praise the Lord! Yes, let's just praise the Lord!

"PRAISE HIM! PRAISE HIM!"

(by Fanny Crosby, public domain)

Praise Him! Praise Him! Jesus, our blessed Redeemer!
Sing, O Earth, His wonderful love proclaim!
Hail Him! Hail Him! Highest archangels in glory;
Strength and honor give to His holy Name!
Like a shepherd, Jesus will guard His children;
In His arms He carries them all day long.

Praise Him! Praise Him! Tell of His excellent greatness;
Praise Him! Praise Him! Ever in joyful song!

Praise Him! Praise Him! Jesus, our blessed Redeemer!
For our sins He suffered, and bled, and died.
He our Rock, our hope of eternal salvation,
Hail Him! Hail Him! Jesus the Crucified.
Sound His praises! Jesus who bore our sorrows,
Love unbounded, wonderful, deep and strong.

Praise Him! Praise Him! Jesus, our blessed Redeemer!
Heav'nly portals loud with hosannas ring!
Jesus, Savior, reigneth forever and ever;
Crown Him! Crown Him! Prophet, and Priest, and King!
Christ is coming, over the world victorious,
Pow'r and glory unto the Lord belong.

ENDNOTES

1. Don Williams, "We Become Like What We Worship," a chapter in Matt Redmon's book, *The Heart of Worship Files* (Ventura, CA: Gospel Light, 2003), 25.

2. Ibid.

3. Matt Redmond, *The Unquenchable Worshipper* (Ventura, CA: Regal Books, 2001), 24.

Chapter Three

OIL FOR PURE WORSHIP

JULIE MEYER

Then the kingdom of heaven shall be likened to ten virgins who took their lamps and went out to meet the bridegroom. Now five of them were wise, and five were foolish. Those who were foolish took their lamps and took no oil with them, but the wise took oil in their vessels with their lamps. But while the bridegroom was delayed, they all slumbered and slept. And at midnight a cry was heard: "Behold, the bridegroom is coming; go out to meet him!" Then all those virgins arose and trimmed their lamps. And the foolish said to the wise, "Give us some of your oil, for our lamps are going out." But the wise answered, saying, "No, lest there should not be enough for us and you; but go rather to those who sell, and buy for yourselves." And while they went to buy, the bridegroom came, and those who were ready went in with him to the wedding; and the door was shut (Matthew 25:1-10 NKJV).

I was invited to Singapore to lead worship for a conference in June 2000. This was my first trip out of the United States and I found myself getting very excited about the sound of our coming worship. The worship team was well-rehearsed; we had gotten a great sound check. We were getting ready to pray together when the pastor came up to me and asked, "Julie, have you ever heard the people worship in this cathedral? Are you prepared to hear a mighty sound arising? The people here sing with all their might. They sing with all their strength; for they have paid a great price to be here. They sing loud, Julie. You will need to tell your team to 'play loud,' because the people will sing louder and overtake you with their singing."

With that, he began to look around the congregation like a father who is expecting the whole family over for Sunday dinner. One by one, he caught the eye of different people and nodded his head as if to say, "We're all here together." I liked him right from the very start. (As I would find out later, he could really preach, too. He had me on the edge of my seat, and I hear a lot of sermons.)

The cathedral was packed full of people from many nations, and they spoke many different languages. I found myself thinking, *Oh, my goodness. I knew I should have studied at least one other language. I know only English.* I began to fret a little, wondering how we would all be able to worship together with so many diverse people groups in attendance.

The guitar began to play; the drums began their rhythm. I remember looking down and placing my fingers on the keys of the piano and, just as I began to sing out that first note of worship, I was literally overtaken by sound. Beautiful sound filled the room, a sound of voices singing with all their hearts to God. Their singing was so loud it was as if I had been hit in the face with a huge wave of sound. It was overpowering. I looked behind me and motioned to the worship team members to play louder. But it was no use. The sound that came from the worshiping people in the congregation engulfed all instruments and seemed to fill every space of the cathedral.

My heart was not prepared for the sound that my ears were hearing, for it was loud and glorious praise to God. The people represented so many different nations, and they were there to worship—to sing out about the glories of their

Lord and Savior. These people were not just passing the time until the speaker would begin. Their words and melodies overtook the musicians and all of us joined together, from the very back of the room to the very front.

The pastor walked over to me again and said, "Julie, do you hear their sound of worship?" He stood there listening, taking in every single note. The harmonies were beautiful, and their voices blended together like artists who have spent many years perfecting their singing.

The pastor said, "Do you see the people on the first seven rows? These are my friends and they are here from Indonesia. I was just there doing the burial ceremony for their pastor who was killed for his faith. Look, Julie; look how they worship the Lord! Listen to their voices. Listen to the strength of their sound. There is no stopping this sound, Julie." Compassion began to fill my heart, and I found myself beginning to tear up as I looked out over this group of people. I just stood there and listened. No leading was necessary as the sound of their voices took over all the space in the room. All eyes were fixed on Jesus.

It was like being in the middle of an ocean of voices. Instead of water, this ocean was filled with waves of sound, and they were arising and crashing down on the worship team. The sound engulfed the whole room.

Then the pastor said one more thing. "Do you know why they sing so loud? Oil. It's oil, Julie. They have a life in God no one would even know about and a reservoir of oil to carry with them wherever they go, regardless of whatever they face or whatever is taken from them. They have an abundance of oil, and it overflows everywhere they go." I looked around the vast cathedral and thought, *This is what a reservoir of oil looks like. When we carry a reservoir of oil within our souls, it bubbles up and it overflows. It spills out into the most powerful of sounds. This is the sound of pure worship.* These people had come together for one purpose, and that purpose was Jesus Christ. They came to lift up His name with the sound of pure worship.

OIL COMES FROM LIFE IN GOD

For me, the lost art of pure worship comes down to one simple question: "Do I have *oil*?" Oil is always one of the most valuable commodities in the earth and it is also the most needed substance for worship.

I believe I saw such pure worship in Singapore because they had the oil.

Oil speaks of our hidden life in God. It is our inward journey with the Holy Spirit, all of the times we are talking to the Holy Spirit and listening to the sound of His voice. It is the way we journey with the Lord in the secret places of our heart where only His eyes gaze. The result is that our hearts become tender, and we begin to feel more of God's love for us. It literally helps us in our journey to choose righteousness. He sees every motive, every intent of our hearts, every choice, every time we forgive, every time we lean into Him, every struggle and every time we choose Him instead of sin or offense. We are always in His gaze and we are always in His heart. He is always encouraging us: "You can do this. I am for you. I will help you. I love you." But we have to do our part and "come away" with Him.

When our hearts are alive in God, and we are talking and singing to God, praising and loving Him when no one is looking, it initiates the spontaneous song that will suddenly spring up in the midst of worship. Suddenly, we burst forth in a new song in the midst of a praise service. Worship is an overflow of what you and I have been doing when we are alone with God—meaning the time we spend during the week cultivating our relationship with the Holy Spirit and Jesus as the Bridegroom God.

We can have a great worship set with beautiful songs, excellent musicians, and no time limits, yet if we have no oil, if we have not taken time to have a heart connection with the Holy Spirit and listen to His voice all week long, then our hearts can be like dry river beds with no running water in sight, and worship can become a "job" instead of an overflow.

But to continually have a heart alive in worship and to walk in a prophetic spirit, we have to have a life *in* God. We must have oil for the journey of worship. The really good news is that our Father loves to give us oil for the journey.

OIL FOR OUR LAMPS

I once had a dream about this oil. It was as if I had stepped right into the parable that I had read and meditated on many times. I was literally inside Matthew 25 as an observer; no one seemed to know I was even there. There was much activity. There was much excitement. There was expectancy in the room.

I noticed that everyone was carrying a lantern, all different kinds of lanterns. Some were very beautiful and some were very simple. Some were very old, and some were new—some so shiny that I found myself marveling at how shiny and unique the lanterns themselves were.

I saw other lanterns not as beautiful or extravagant as others in the room. Suddenly, instead of the outsides of the lanterns, my eye fell upon the oil on the insides. Some of the lanterns were full. They were so full that there was oil running down the outside, and this oil had a fragrance that seemed to rise clear past the ceiling itself. I saw that some of the most mundane-looking lanterns actually contained the *most* oil and some of the most beautiful ones had the *least*. I thought to myself, *Don't be fooled by someone's pretty lamp—it is what is on the inside that counts.*

The hour became late and everyone began to sleep. Suddenly, when all was still and silent, *"at the midnight hour,"* when we least expected it, we all heard a cry: *"Behold, the Bridegroom cometh!"*

Now everyone in the room woke up, and they began to get ready very quickly. They all got up and readied their lamps so that they could go out into the night and meet the Bridegroom.

That is when a great struggle began, for many people had beautiful lanterns but they did not have oil. Each of them had a lamp. Their lamps spoke of ministries that bring light to others. Everyone had a lamp; everyone had a ministry. They all went out to encounter Jesus as the Bridegroom. The foolish took their lamps but they *took no oil,* meaning they were pursuing ministry as their priority over getting oil. The wise *took oil* in their vessels with their lamps, for they pursued oil as their priority before ministry. I saw that oil was literally the most important thing. Without oil, nobody could have a shining light. Without a reservoir of oil, the light could not be sustained.

For you and me, the key for sustaining our shine is to carry a reservoir of oil within ourselves. How do we develop our reservoir of oil? That is easy; we simply must develop a heart connection with the Holy Spirit and Jesus the Bridegroom God. We simply make time for God. We need to let the Holy Spirit into our lives on every level, all the time.

This oil is every "yes" that we ever say to God when no one is looking. This oil represents all that is done in secret when it is just you or me and God alone. Every single time you make a choice for God, it is as if oil is being multiplied within your soul. That oil overflows in every season of your life, including the unexpected "midnight suddenlies" of God.

No one can take this from us, and we cannot give this away; for though many people shine, no one can *sustain* the shine without oil, without a secret life in God.

I woke up from the dream and I thought, *I need more oil. Capture every thought, Jesus, let every beat of my heart beat for You. Let every syllable and every word belong to You. Jesus, let me love You with the words of my mouth. Jesus, let me love You with the mediation of my thoughts. This is oil and I need more.*

My thoughts went back to the year 2000 and to the words that the pastor had spoken to me. "It is oil, Julie. Some of these people do not know if they will be alive tomorrow or if their families will be alive tomorrow. Still, they walk with God every day. They talk to the Holy Spirit every day." I remembered the sound of their loud and beautiful worship as it filled that cathedral. I knew that those people had the "shine" that comes from having the oil.

BUY OIL

Many of us have "shine" for the moment; we have enough oil for today. But when tomorrow comes, our lamps are dry. God is inviting us, as worshipers, as prophetic musicians, prophetic singers, to get more oil.

The foolish say, "Give us some of your oil, for ours is gone." They are really saying, "Our shine is beginning to go out. Our divine influence has gone out. I do not know His voice anymore. I have been busy in ministry, I have been busy practicing and leading worship, yet I have not spent time in His presence to know His voice. I don't know His voice anymore; please tell me what He is saying."

Now practicing and leading worship are good, but no one can have a heart overflowing with pure worship without oil. The lover in the Song of Solomon says, "Draw me after you and we will run together" (see Song of Sol. 1:4). We have to let our hearts be drawn away with the Lord more than we run with Him. We cannot run first and expect our hearts to be drawn away second. We need to keep the first things first. It is all in having a relationship with the Lord. It is having more than just a pretty lamp, having more than just a nice ministry; it is having a relationship with the Holy Spirit. It is getting oil.

When we read the story in Matthew 25, we see that the foolish virgins were told to go *buy* oil. That word *buy* is *agorazo* in Greek, and it is the same word that is used in Revelation 3:18:

> *I counsel you to **buy** from Me gold refined in the fire, that you may be rich; and white garments, that you may be clothed, that the shame of your nakedness may not be revealed...* (Revelation 3:18 NKJV).

This word means to get or acquire something from God Himself. Nobody else can give us what we need. Nobody can give us their history in God or their relationship with the Holy Spirit, so they cannot give us their oil. Each of us has our own journey with the Lord, and it takes work to get oil.

And when we hear "Behold, the Bridegroom cometh," it is *not* the right time to get oil. For the sound of this cry is like a trumpet. Something is up. This is the time to *have* oil and not the time to go buy oil. This is the "suddenly" of God. (This parable describes the return of Christ, but it has many layers; one of the layers is about having oil and being ready for the "suddenlies" of God to arise.)

We need to have filled our lamps with oil ahead of time. The Holy Spirit is inviting us to get oil, to buy gold, to get wisdom, to hear the new song, to sing the new song, to seek Him daily. He is freely giving oil out to those who will "buy" it by seeking for it.

"Seek the Lord while He may be found, call upon Him while He is near" (Isa. 55:6 NKJV). *"Draw near to God and He will draw near to you..."* (James 4:8 NKJV).

He *will* draw near. We were created by God and for God. We were created to love God and to feel His love. Through Jesus, He has made it possible for us to come to Him and talk with Him.

God has His fingers on the worship movement in the earth. He longs for a sound to be released that is full of the passion of who He is, a beautiful sound arising and revealing the depths of His love, the greatness of His power, and the beauty of Jesus the Bridegroom God.

If you want to be a true worshiper, a prophetic worshiper, you must have oil. It doesn't work if all you have is a pretty lamp. You cannot impart something in worship that you do not have for yourself. But our awesome Jesus has made it so easy, because oil comes as we walk and talk with God—day by day, step by step, choice by choice, and yes by yes. It is that simple.

What does your life look like? That is the story God has created. He wants to meet you in the midst of it, to give you oil in the place where you find yourself—and to become the center of your praise.

King David is such a great example of a worshiper. He looked for God everywhere. He talked to God always. David's heart was fixed upon God and he sang to the Lord at all times. We can see this throughout the psalms.

David spoke to the Lord the words of this song on the day that the Lord delivered him from the hand of his enemies and from the hand of Saul: "[You] *delivered me because* [You, God] *delighted in me....For who is God, except the Lord? And who is a rock, except our God? It is God who arms me with strength...*" (Ps. 18:19, 31-32 NKJV).

We find in this portion of Scripture that David is declaring, "Lord, because You delight in me, You deliver me." I love this about King David. David was called a man after God's own heart because he studied and understood the emotions of God. That is why he would run *to* God instead of running away from Him in his weakness. He can say, "God, because You take extravagant joy over my life, You, God, will deliver me. *I am Your favorite* even in my weakness!"

David just said "yes" to God. The simplicity of getting oil is saying "yes" when most of the time no one even notices. This simple "yes" is the very beginning step in learning to cultivate a relationship with the Holy Spirit and Jesus as the Bridegroom God. This is the place where we begin to feel and understand His love for us. It is not just head knowledge and a memorized Scripture, but we actually experience His love. This will greatly change our worship, and we literally become the melody that He sings through us. We begin to know the sound of His voice. We learn how to listen to what He is saying. We know what is on His heart, and that is the oil that will overflow in the midst of worship.

The Holy Spirit deep inside of us is always searching out the depths of God and revealing His thoughts to us. We simply sing it out. When the Spirit of the Lord was poured out on the day of Pentecost (see Acts 2), God threw away the measuring cup. He gave us *all* of His Spirit. I believe the purpose of our journey in this life is to get to know Him, to learn the sound of His voice, to "get oil," to pursue a relationship with the Holy Spirit and Jesus the Bridegroom God more than we pursue "ministry."

As worshipers, we must turn every situation we go through into an opportunity to get oil. Even in seasons of promotion or demotion, seasons when we are overlooked and we have no favor, we should say, "Don't get offended...get oil!" As another psalm puts it, "Promotion does not come from the south, east, or west; it comes from God. God raises one up and presses one down" (see Ps. 75:6-7).

You cannot get oil and be offended at the same time. The two do not meet up. One will win. And it is always easier to be offended. Remember: offense never lets you go—you have to let it go. Sometimes it is just a little thing, but other times it is really big things.

DON'T GET OFFENDED—GET OIL

I was invited to lead worship in another country. With a team of musicians and singers from the church, I would lead the people in worship and intercession every night for five nights. The congregation would be singing and praying for their nation. I was so excited to hear the sound of their singing and to hear the people begin to pray for God to arise in their nation. Now, their cultural style of worship was very different from mine. The worship leader and the singers would all line up on stage and dance around on the platform, encouraging all in the congregation to sing. It was a lot of fun with a lot of joy but very different from my style of worship. (There is no right or wrong style of worship—just different.) So when I stood behind the keyboard to lead in a different way, it was very new to the worship team.

After the second night, the worship pastor was driving me home, and he said something that gave me a wonderful opportunity to not be offended. He told me, "Julie, our worship team called a meeting and we have taken a vote. We have firmly decided that we are unimpressed with your worship leading." Then he told me who the team had voted was their favorite American worship leader.

Well, what do you say to that? I was thinking to myself, *Remember what you always say—Go low; don't get offended or angry.* But I was quite shocked, and I found myself saying, "You actually called a meeting and you all took a vote about my worship leading?"

Again he said, "Yes, and we have all *firmly decided* we are unimpressed with your worship leading." Well, I did not know what to say. That had never happened to me before. I could not believe what I had heard. I started getting a bit frustrated (that is the Christian way to say I was really ticked), and certain thoughts ran through my mind, like, *Well, you are a boring preacher and all of your kids are ugly.*

I really did think those thoughts. My goodness, I thought I had oil. I thought my love for Jesus and my understanding of what He did for me on the cross meant that I could just love and love some more. But at that moment I just wanted to strike.

To calm my emotions, I actually did a couple of the Lamaze breathing exercises that I had used in childbirth! In spite of the wrestling match going on inside my heart, I said, "Well, I do not know what to say. I am sorry but I am not trying to impress anyone. I was invited to come over here across the ocean and to lead a people in prayer and worship. If I have not done that, I am greatly sorry."

We drove the rest of the way home in silence. I was realizing that we still had three nights of worship left, and somehow I would have to lead a team of *unimpressed* musicians and singers. That seemed like such a bizarre statement. I got out of the car and kind of waved good-bye to the worship pastor while beginning to pray inside, "I love You, Jesus. You love me, Jesus. I am here for You and You alone. Help my heart right now to forgive. Help my heart right now to choose life and to choose You. Help me to be able to go in that sanctuary tomorrow night and lead another night of worship with an unoffended heart. Help me to love this team like You, Jesus, would love this team."

The wonderful part of this whole wrestling match inside me was the fact that I had spent time over the years cultivating a relationship with the Holy Spirit. Right in that moment, I began to hear the Holy Spirit speak to me: *Julie, go low; do not get offended.* I knew the sound of His voice. I knew He was speaking to me. When you have touched His love in the secret place, His voice is impossible to ignore. Holding onto offense is not an option, because I love Him, and because He loves me.

And right there, before my hand even touched the latch of the front door, I felt the love of Jesus come in and flood my soul. I knew that He was with me and that He had my back. I knew that I was there to love and that if I did my part, the Spirit of God would come and soften hearts and turn every gaze to the Man truly deserving of all our worship.

The next night, He was greatly at work inside my heart and emotions. I arrived just before the service started; to make matters worse, the person scheduled to pick me up had forgotten, so I arrived just in time for the service to begin and was not able to talk to the worship team. I still remember the angry faces of the worship team as I walked up to the piano. I remember hearing the opening prayer and thinking, *OK, God, this is just You and me.* Under my breath, I began to say, "You love the sound of our worship. You love the sound of our voices. You never get tired of the sound of our worship. This is to You and for You, Jesus."

With that, I put my hands slowly upon the keyboard and began to sing, "Here I am to worship. Here I am to bow down. Here I am to say that You're my God...." As I began to sing, the whole congregation joined in singing immediately, as they were unaware of the struggle happening with the worship team. The whole room chimed in with that sweet chorus. Throughout the service, I just sang about His beauty and His deep love. There was a tender presence of the Holy Spirit in the room as He began to soften the hearts of everyone, including the worship team.

The next night, I arrived to see everyone's heart a little more tender. Small, faint smiles were beginning to replace faces of anger, and the walls that seemed to divide two different cultures of worship began to fall. You just cannot help but run straight into His love and forgiveness when all eyes are on the King of Kings. By the last evening, the worship team was in tears, and the love of Jesus flooded the sanctuary. After the meeting was over, there were lots of tears and lots of hugs and lots of joy and smiles.

This was a great lesson for me to learn. As I left the building that night, my mind went back to the experience in Singapore years before. For those were the worshipers who were unoffended, and they sang their vow of unwavering devotion to Jesus. They had a reservoir of oil that spilled over to me and set me on a journey to develop a deeper inner life with the Holy Spirit.

Then my thoughts went to my last five days, where I had had the opposite experience. For I was the one with the oil that began to spill out to the worshipers in the room and they began to cry out for a deeper heart connection with the Spirit and Jesus as the Bridegroom God. The oil, the history in God that I carried, the affection of Jesus, spilled out of my life onto them, and they began their own journey of getting oil.

As a worshiper, the lost art of pure worship comes down to one thing: oil. And He is near, with an invitation to all. Pursue a relationship with the Holy Ghost and Jesus the Bridegroom God *more than* ministry. For if we know Him, everything else will fall precisely into place. He wants to use our song and our worship to invite everyone to gaze on the beauty of His face—and get oil.

ALABASTER BOX

(© Julie Meyer)

All I am, is all I have
And all, all I have to give.
Lord, I give it all to You.
It's my fragrant oil,
It's my costly perfume.
I take my Alabaster Box and I break it open.
Let the fragrance arise ... la la la la... la la la la
So I pour out my worship over You;
I sing my song of worship straight to You.

Section Two

EQUAL ACCESS
TO THE THRONE

Therefore, since we have a great high priest who has passed through the heavens, Jesus the Son of God, let us hold fast our confession. For we do not have a high priest who cannot sympathize with our weaknesses, but One who has been tempted in all things as we are, yet without sin. Therefore let us draw near with confidence to the throne of grace, so that we may receive mercy and find grace to help in time of need (Hebrews 4:14-16 NASB).

Through His shed blood and the completed work on the cross, Jesus has once and for all time made the way to the Father and the presence of the Holy Spirit. Each one of us can now enter in. Through Jesus, we can draw near to the throne of the Almighty and receive grace and mercy.

You do not have to be from an elite family or of a special ethnic origin to come into God's equal-access presence. You do not have to be of a specific gender or belong to a certain age group. You can come into His courts with thanksgiving and into His gates through the power of praise. It requires only a simple posture of the heart.

Let us draw near with confidence to the throne of grace.

Chapter Four

TABERNACLE OF DAVID

CHRIS DUPRÉ

We owe our present-day expression of worship to a young man who helped usher in a radical change in the way worship was defined and demonstrated. Though the youngest of a large family, he was able to be his own man and develop his own authentic and personal relationship with the Lord. With a tender heart and remarkable musical skills, he blazed a way for all worshipers to follow.

King David was a man for his time and a man ahead of his time. So much of what we do in the arena of worship has come from him. Without David, our conversations about worship would end up using words like blood, sacrifice, knife, dead, wash, splattered, animal...you get the picture.

God's initial intent was for men and women to walk in the Garden with Him. He wanted to converse with them; His goal was to have an intimate relationship with the human beings He had created. That was lost when sin entered the picture. For thousands of years people continued to live, work, and (unfortunately) worship outside of that place of intimacy. It was only when David came on the scene that things began to change.

David was a different kind of kid. When King Saul disobeyed the Lord and offered his wrongful sacrifice, God began to look for someone else to lead His people. In the prophet Samuel's search for a new king, he was led to the house of Jesse, David's father. Samuel went through Jesse's lineup of sons, but did not choose any of them. (See First Samuel 16.) Finally Jesse remembered that he had one more son, his youngest son David, a young, singing shepherd who spent his days watching sheep and worshiping on the hillside. They sent for him. When David came through the doorway, Samuel immediately heard the Lord say, *"Rise and anoint him; this is the one"* (1 Sam. 16:12). Samuel took his horn of oil and anointed David in the midst of his brothers.

AFTER GOD'S OWN HEART

Why did God choose David? What made him so special? We can find an answer in the statement that Samuel made when he was chastising Saul for his disobedience. He had said that God was seeking for someone *"after His own heart"* (1 Sam. 13:14). David was special because he was that someone who was "after God's own heart."

For years I assumed that this statement had to do with how fervently David pursued God, and that to have a heart "after" God spoke of passionate pursuit, like a runner after the prize. This made sense to me, because as a young man I had run track, and I fully understand what it means to run after something. The more gifted the runner, the more rewarded he becomes.

For me, this translated after I was saved into a lifestyle of "doing" for God. To have a heart "after" God, I felt I must be running after Him with as much effort as possible in my pursuit of ministry and purpose. Needless to say, this kind of thinking and activity has a limited shelf life.

It was only after many years that I began to realize that my pursuit of God was not yielding the kind of inner peace that I longed for. I was always running into my imperfections, which left me short of my desired goal. But then something happened to help me realize that I had been wrong about my understanding of the word "after" in the phrase, "a man after God's own heart."

I was at a wedding when I overheard an older lady praise a little boy for his politeness. He was all dressed up and standing next to his father. She said to the boy's father, "Oh my, he really does take after you." Shortly thereafter I heard the same type of comment from someone else. Then it hit me: that's what "after" means!

Naturally, I had been using a running definition for "after," but that wasn't what it meant. The word actually means leaning toward or reflecting another's image or having similar attributes to another. Another translation makes the meaning of that line clearer: God calls David a man *"according* to My own heart."

When God was searching for another leader after Saul sinned, He was looking for someone who had a heart that reflected His own heart. He wanted a leader who had a heart so similar to His heart that, through that man's leadership, His intentions and desires would be seen and realized.

When you have a heart after God, it does not consign you to a lifestyle of running headlong after God, in hopes that one day you will finally catch Him. Instead, having a heart after God means that you know and understand God's heart and you therefore live your life knowing He loves and desires you. Out of a place of peace, you become a reflection of His light, love, and glory.

So the definition of your being "a man after God's own heart" is not trying to catch up with God, but rather it is knowing that you have already caught Him—or, better yet, He has already caught you.

RESTORING THE TABERNACLE OF DAVID

An incredible verse of promise in the Book of Amos has become very popular recently. It reads, *"On that day I will raise up the tabernacle of David, which has fallen down, and repair its damages; I will raise up its ruins, and rebuild it as in the days of old"* (Amos 9:11 NKJV).

Because of this verse, we have seen a resurgence in the past few years of teaching about the tabernacle of David.

To many, it speaks directly of the promise to restore Israel to a place of honor, power, and relationship with God. That may be true, but with the incredible growth of the present worldwide prayer movement, many teachings today seem to emphasize a different perspective. Today's teachings focus more on certain questions, such as: "How did David set up the tabernacle and how did the worship and prayer movement of that time really work?" Also, "What does that past time and experience have to do with my life today?"

These are good questions, but answering them (and others like them) has started to make us zero in on God's revelation about other aspects of David's tabernacle. We have started to pose a new question: "With Amos 9:11 promising restoration of David's tabernacle, what exactly is it that God wants to restore?"

The answer becomes one of the most important truths we need to know. To get there it's probably best to go back and see what David's tabernacle was all about.

After Samuel anointed him and after much time and tribulation, David had been made king over Judah, but as Judah was only one of the 12 tribes, his power was limited. His desire to restore the ark of the covenant and to reign in Jerusalem would have to wait until after the death of Saul.

Shortly after Saul's death, the leaders of all the tribes of Israel gathered together in Hebron and made David king over all 12 tribes. David soon attacked the Jebusites who were entrenched in Jerusalem, drove them out, and took Jerusalem as his home city. Soon thereafter, Jerusalem started to be called, appropriately, the City of David.

Here we have David, finally in power over all of Israel (see 1 Chron. 11), and the first thing he wanted to do was to bring the ark of the covenant back home.

David understood its importance, and he knew that it had not been sought after during the time of Saul. Now he made a priority of restoring the ark to its rightful place, Jerusalem.

David began by consulting with the leaders, saying, *"If it seems good to you, and if it is of the Lord our God, let us...bring the ark of our God back to us..."* (1 Chron. 13:2-3 NKJV). That sounds really good—but David never did consult the Lord about it. He consulted only with the leaders and he hoped that God would go along with his good idea.

The idea to bring back the ark of the covenant was not a bad idea. The problem lay in how David decided to go about it. He should have known that it needed to be "handled with care." The whole time it had been in the hands of the Philistines, it had only caused them trouble. (Remember the story about Dagon in First Samuel 5?) They were glad to be rid of it, and it was now awaiting them in Kiriath Jearim. David's desire for the ark was not the problem; it was in how he wanted to carry God's presence.

Instead of God's prescribed method, being carried on the shoulders of the Levites, David chose the Philistine's method, which was putting the ark on a new cart and having oxen pull the cart. That seemed to David to be the most convenient and practical way of moving the ark. What he did not seem to be aware of was God's stated desire to have His presence carried only by people. God did not want carts and oxen because they would always turn out to be diversions that would get in the way of His people's face-to-face relationship with Him.

Well, David soon learned that truth when in the midst of singing and dancing, as the ark was being transported, the oxen stumbled, a man named Uzzah put his hand out to steady the ark and, upon touching it, he was struck dead instantly. The ark was taken to Obed-Edom's house where it stayed for three months while David tried to figure out what had gone wrong.

Soon enough, he tried again. This time, he did it God's way:

After David had constructed buildings for himself in the City of David, he prepared a place for the ark of God and pitched a tent for it. Then David said, "No one but the Levites may carry the ark of God, because the Lord chose them to carry the ark of the Lord and to minister before Him forever" (1 Chronicles 15:1-2).

This time, the ark was carried on the shoulders of the Levites, which had been God's intention from the beginning. God always wants to be with people and to move with people as they move with Him. Oxen are fine for the world's work, but when God wants to move with humans, all He wants is Him and us. No carts, no oxen. Oxen and carts are for work, not for worship.

EQUAL ACCESS

David was successful in returning the ark to Jerusalem but then he had another situation to deal with. Up until that time, the ark's final resting place had always been inside the Holy of Holies, where no one but the high priest would ever look upon it. The high priest had the great honor of being the only one who could enter the Holy of Holies where the ark of the covenant rested, and he entered only on one day of the year, the Day of Atonement. God's instructions for the high priest were very clear (see Lev. 16 and Exod. 30:6-10). First, he always needed to go through an elaborate sanctifying ritual, and he needed to wear bells on the bottom of his garments and a rope around his leg as he entered, because the least little uncovered sin or unfinished ritual of sanctification would render him lifeless and he would need to be dragged from the Most Holy Place. (Ah, what a job!)

Now David comes along and changes all that, saying, "Hey, I have pitched a tent and I want to put the ark of the covenant right in the middle of it and worship the Lord day and night. Is anybody with me?"

I can hear the people shouting, "Yes, David. We're with you! You're the man! We're with you all the way!" And then if you listen in a little closer, you can hear the people whispering, "Is he crazy? We'll all die if he puts the ark out in the open. For the last 1,000 years only the high priest could be exposed to the ark and, even then, only once a year. David wants us all to be exposed to it, every hour of every day. What is he thinking? Oh, God, please help us!"

In actuality, David was an incredible leader, and he always looked after the most important things first. After he took his role as king over all Israel, the first thing he had done was to build a house for himself (see 1 Chron. 15). Some might think that this was ego-driven, but in truth it shows how a good leader will plant himself in the middle of where he's leading so that others will do the same. The minute David built a house for himself, others would look and say, "If David is putting down roots here, then so will I."

Next, David put others into their God-ordained places of ministry and leadership. (See, for example, First Chronicles 15:16-24.) As he did so, David released them to be true leaders by giving them the authority to recruit and appoint others to places of leadership.

Many times over the years I have been in the position to appoint someone into a new place of ministry. It is one of my greatest joys to see people released to do what they long to and are called to do. Sometimes, though, it can be tough for certain people to accept decisions I've made concerning others. One of the greatest windows into someone's heart is seeing their ability or inability to rejoice when someone else moves ahead with the favor of God. Many are quick to weep with those who weep but find it very difficult to rejoice with those who rejoice.

Though I always try to look mainly at the person's heart, I also look for a level of ability and excellence in musicians. Sloppy musicianship is often a red flag for a sloppy lifestyle. David understood this; we see him putting Kenaniah in charge of all the singing because he was skillful at it (see 1 Chron. 15:22). The account doesn't say he was the *most* skillful, but we do see that David was moving in wisdom when he put a very skilled man in charge because he must have carried that wonderful combination of heart and skill.

From his earliest time during Saul's rule as king, David had been known as a man of music and worship. Whenever he would strum his instrument and begin to sing, evil spirits would flee, unable to deal with the worship-initiated increase of God's Spirit. David's life was all about the desire for more of the presence of God and singing was a huge part. "Sing unto the Lord" was a phrase that he would use over and over in his life, not in a religious way, but as a way to connect his heart with the heart of God.

Because of this, he introduced a completely new expression of worship to the people of Israel. They had always been a musical people (remember Miriam's song in Exodus 15), but David took it to a whole new level. From his time forward, music was not only to be part of Jewish culture—now, because of David, it was to be part of Jewish *worship*. The specifics of what we call Davidic worship were not new to the daily life of the people; it's just that now they were to be a major part of their ongoing expression of worship to God.

David instituted a whole new way of life for the people of Israel, one that included singing, musical instruments, praise, rejoicing, clapping, shouting, dancing, lifting of hands, bowing, and a myriad of other wonderful actions, both of the heart and of the body. He was making sure that God would receive all of the worship and praise that He was due.

And a funny thing happened when the people were all gathered before the ark and exposed to the presence of God...no one died! In fact, for most of them, this provided their first chance to really live as God had ordained them to live, in a vital, ongoing, worshipful relationship with their God.

HOW SHOULD THE TABERNACLE OF DAVID BE RESTORED?

These days, our newly discovered understanding of the tabernacle of David has led some of us to want to recapture those great years when David was king and his house of worship and prayer were going great guns.

I'm not speaking against any part of the current worship or prayer movement. I was a part of the early years in the International House of Prayer in Kansas City. I saw the purity of heart that went into creating 84 two-hour prayer sessions per week. Unfortunately, though, I have been in places where what some people want to do is to go backward in their form and expression of worship to a bygone day of butterflies, sunshine, and "all's right with the world." It didn't exist then and it doesn't exist now.

As we see in the fifteenth chapter of Acts, certain people were teaching new believers that unless they were circumcised according to the Law of Moses, they could not be saved. This created a sharp dispute, so a gathering was called together in Jerusalem to discuss the matter with the apostles. At the meeting, Peter, Paul, and Barnabas spoke concerning the need to allow the Gentiles to come into the Kingdom unburdened, but it was James who brought the decisive word of the Lord. He quoted from the prophet Amos: *"After this I will return and rebuild David's fallen tent. Its ruins I will rebuild, and I will restore it, **that the rest of mankind may seek the Lord, even all the Gentiles who bear My name...**"* (Acts 15:16-17).

These words say nothing about music or even worship. They speak of David's tabernacle being rebuilt, but there isn't a word about a worship leader or an anointed worship team. No singer or instrumentalist is ever mentioned. That's because what God intended to restore from David's tabernacle was what He was most interested in from the beginning regarding David's tabernacle, and music was only part of it.

David had put the ark right in the middle of the tabernacle because David knew God's heart. He knew God loved music and singing, but he also knew that what God was most interested in was allowing people to have complete and unhindered access to Him. God's initial intent had been to walk face-to-face, side-by-side with Adam in the Garden. David felt the heartbeat of God and helped orchestrate His plan to once again put God and His presence right in the middle of His people.

When the council in Jerusalem met to discuss the situation of the new Gentile believers, James rightly pointed out God's intent for the tabernacle of David. Salvation and all life in Him is not for only some people, it's for all! No walls, no veils, no restrictions! God wants to be available, *"that the rest of mankind may seek the Lord, even all the Gentiles"* Acts 15:17.

Now it was time to rebuild David's tabernacle. Not with human hands, for God had said, *"...I will rebuild, and I will restore it..."* (Acts 15:16). Yes, a new and exciting worship movement was going on, but something greater was happening—God was revealing His heart to the world when David put the ark of the covenant right in the middle so that everyone would have access to Him.

As most of us know, David is a "type" of Christ. He represents the kingly role of Jesus as well as Jesus' priestly role. David was king of Judah for seven years and then he became king over all Israel. He reigned for a total of 40 years.

The tabernacle of David was present only during David's reign as king of Israel. When you subtract the seven years David reigned as king of Judah from his total reign, you get the number of years that the tabernacle of David was in existence. Forty years minus 7 years equals 33 years; the tabernacle of David existed for 33 years.

Thirty-three years...Hmm. That number points to the way God wanted to reveal through David's tabernacle an even greater example of access to God. For the same length of time—33 years—Jesus Himself, the very Son of God, walked this earth to declare that, whoever would believe in Him would have eternal life. Paul wrote, *"For through Him* [Jesus] *we both* [Jews and Gentiles] *have **access** to the Father by one Spirit"* (Eph. 2:18). There it is again...access.

That was God's plan all along. If the greatest worship or prayer movement in the world doesn't provide access to God, it is not of His heart. Outward forms of expression tend to supersede the work of the heart, and that is never God's intent. Remember, when God was searching for a man to take Saul's place, He was looking not on David's outward actions and qualifications, but rather He was looking at his heart.

Jesus came; He rent the veil. There is no longer anything keeping us from God. As He said, *"I will never leave you nor forsake you"* (Heb. 13:5 NKJV; see also Deut. 31:6). Often our hearts, even our prayers and songs, ignore this wonderful truth and seem to express the heart of an orphan, imploring Him to come when, in reality, He has never left.

I have no problem with praying for more of Him. One of my favorite Vineyard songs goes like this, "More love, more power, more of You in my life." That is not a song from a depressed heart that feels abandoned by God. Rather, the song acknowledges our weakness and our constant need of Him. I am more concerned with the prayers and songs that sound as if God has gone away, and that if we pray hard enough and long enough (and sometimes loud enough), then He will hear us, feel sorry for us, and come to our rescue. *We need to know, deeply know, that God has **never** left us and that He never will.*

David's tabernacle spoke of eternal access to God; Jesus reiterated that He would never leave us nor forsake us; and the wonderful promise of God's Spirit is a testament of His abiding presence in our lives.

Worship is most free when it comes from a free heart. A heart that has unlimited access to God has a free choice. The person can choose to draw near or choose to go his or her own way. When you choose Him, you have chosen well. You can then rest in the fact that He loves you perfectly and, as any father would, loves to have His children choose to run to Him because they know that He is good.

He is here for you...always!

He is available for you...always!

He is waiting for you...always!

AS A SEAL UPON MY HEART

(© Chris DuPré)

As a seal upon my heart
Set Your love, O Lord
For I am Your bride.
As a seal upon my heart
Set Your love, O Lord
And let me lean upon Your side.
For love is strong as death.
With a fire, waters cannot quench.
Love is stronger than the grave
So come and fan the flame
That burns within my soul.

Chapter Five

TWENTY-FOUR/SEVEN

SEAN FEUCHT

During the first year and initial launch of the grassroots Burn 24-7 movement out of my dorm room in Tulsa, Oklahoma, we were anything but organized or "on the map" with other prayer and worship organizations around the world. We did not yet have 501(c)(3) nonprofit status or a legitimate Website, and we were still trying to decide if the name "Burn" would just scare people into thinking we were some weird arsonist cult! Oh yes, and this was also before Facebook was on the scene.

This is why I was surprised one day to receive a call on my cell phone from one of the leading producers of MTV in New York City. He said that he had somehow heard of a group of wild, grassroots believers calling themselves "the Burn," who apparently were gathering in cities across the nation for all-night worship and prayer meetings. He was astounded that teens and 20-somethings would forgo the weekend nightlife of drugs, sex, and partying in favor of sitting in a room with a handful of "radicals" (as he called them), singing hymns and liturgical prayers. When I explained to him that it wasn't exactly "hymns and liturgical prayers," but more like "strumming-three-chords-while-pouring-your-heart-out-to-God," he was even more enthralled.

After talking for a bit and explaining what our little movement (only ten cities at the time) was all about, I finally began to ask him a few questions. Why had he even called in the first place? How could he have been searching for some grassroots, radical, no-name group such as ours? What did he have to gain by finding my number (which I found a bit creepy) and asking me these questions in the midst of his busy and illustrious career as a producer of some of MTV's hottest shows? His responses simply blew my mind and rearranged my perspective.

He told me that his job was to get a pulse on what was feeding this hunger and renaissance of young people praying and worshiping across America. He said that there had been a "very vocal" outcry from their viewers for more information on this "Jesus frenzy." He gave me the example of their yearly poll where thousands and thousands of subscribers note their top priorities and interests for the coming season of programs. This poll largely steers their programming development. This producer then told me that for three years running, the number one requested topic by subscribers worldwide had been the desire to know more about God! Can you believe it?

There is a hungry stirring in the hearts of people all across the world to know, feel, and experience the presence of God. They are not looking for the next catchy church program or religious trapping, but rather a quest for authenticity. It drives them. Worship ushers in the atmosphere they crave.

We are called to carry, embody, and release worship everywhere we go. As the breathing, living, mobile New Testament tabernacle of David, we are the resting place of His presence.

TWENTY-SEVEN/FOUR COMES BEFORE TWENTY-FOUR/SEVEN

Not only are we seeing a worldwide restoration of the tabernacle of David (see Amos 9:11; Acts 15:16) and a wildfire of 24-7 worship and prayer across virtually every nation on earth, but also God is awakening the heart of David in His people. This is not a lust for the limelight or the drive to be up on a platform, but rather the call of a simple shepherd boy who developed a deep, personal heart for worship while he was tending his father's sheep. It was from his deep reservoir of intimacy with God that he penned these words that are now an anthem to an entire generation of worshipers:

> *One thing I ask from the Lord, this only do I seek: that I may dwell in the house of the Lord all the days of my life, to gaze on the beauty of the Lord and to seek Him in His temple* (Psalm 27:4).

By cultivating intimacy with God, David got prepared for the giants, battles, betrayals, and victories to come. In the same way, the depth of the intimacy of any generation of people will determine the scope of their authority on the earth. I believe God is calling forth a true apostolic worship movement that will flood the earth, fill the nations with His presence, and establish the dominion of Jesus to invade a broken humanity. This must be birthed in the secret place, and there are no shortcuts. The reviving of the secret places will always lead to the reviving of the public places.

What was King David's goal in establishing the first tabernacle that was meant purely for worship (and did not require blood sacrifices)? It was not to fulfill some religious obligation regarding 24-7-365 worship. The goal was communion with the Father, intimacy with God. The perpetual 24-7-365 worship happened simply as an outward manifestation of an inward reality. It's still true today; 24-7 worship will always be preceded by David's heartfelt prayer in Psalm 27:4. This "One Thing" intimacy is the ignition point for the explosion of the worldwide worship movement.

ELEVEN/ELEVEN

Besides "27:4" and "24:7," I have been seeing the numbers "11:11" and "1:11" virtually every day for the past two years. I see them on license plates, clocks, billboards, flight numbers, hotel room numbers, and even food expiration dates. It has gone beyond the status of "weird" into the status of "annoying!" I don't think it's some quirky charismatic spoof, because many prophetic leaders across the Body of Christ have talked about noticing 11:11 and 1:11 a lot, too.

What does it mean? Among many meanings, I believe these numbers speak specifically of (1) transition, (2) alignment, and (3) the birth of a new sound. We can see this taking place on a personal level as many people are relocating and acquiring new jobs, as well as in the great "shakings" that are removing whatever hinders people from pursuing their ordained callings. We can also see it taking place on a corporate level within the global Church. Widespread recalibration is in effect, accompanied by a tangible grace to reprioritize vision and mission—and not revert back to the way things have always been done. Many churches and ministries are experiencing a total overhaul in preparation for the season ahead.

This transition is from "programs" to "presence," from Saul to David, from Martha to Mary, from obligation to fascination, and from balance to fullness. It comes with a new sound of worship, praise, and adoration that cannot be classified, contained, or controlled. This intense sound carries Heaven's confirmation and authority and releases freedom as we have never seen before, ushering in the greatest days in the history of the Church. As the song from the mouths of Paul and Silas in Acts 16 caused shackles to fall off and prison doors to break wide open, so will this rising roar of worship from the Bride of Christ break strongholds, oppression, and fear off entire nations and people groups.

Among the many 11:11 and 1:11 Bible verses I have meditated on throughout the past year (including Deuteronomy 11:11, Proverbs 11:11, Psalm 111:1, Isaiah 1:11, Luke 11:11, John 11:11, Hebrews 11:11, and more), there is none more timely than Malachi 1:11. The words from this prophet of old validate and expound on this transition into worship-based living:

"My name will be great among the nations, from where the sun rises to where it sets. In every place incense and pure offerings will be brought to Me, because My name will be great among the nations," says the Lord Almighty (Malachi 1:11).

Malachi envisioned a day when pure incense offerings would rise from "every place" and flood the atmosphere of the earth. This incense is the global sound of day and night worship. During the past few decades, we have witnessed a dramatic and unprecedented acceleration toward the fulfillment of this prophetic word.

This transformational worship sound is not restricted to traditional Sunday morning church gatherings or stale, sparsely attended Wednesday night prayer meetings. The awakening of the Bride in the presence of her Bridegroom is resulting in a barrage of worship coming from everywhere—the slums, street corners, red light districts, suburbs, cafés, and prayer rooms all over the world. This sound is extending far beyond the walls of the church and it is breaking open even the hardest ground and the darkest hearts. "Every place" will surely be saturated with this sound! The sacred is invading the secular in a mighty overflow of love, affection, and passion from every nation on the face of the earth.

OUR CURRENT REALITY

What an hour to be alive! What a privilege to be a part of this planet-shaking, world-altering move of His presence! Many days, I wake up in the morning and pinch myself to verify that this is reality; we live in the very days that the prophets and apostles of old predicted with holy excitement and godly jealousy in their spirits. The words Jesus spoke to His disciples in private, after pulling them away from the outbreak of miracles, reverberate in my spirit: *"Blessed are the eyes that see what you see"* (Luke 10:23).

Isaiah foresaw a time in which "all nations" would join in the song, and their indigenous expressions of worship would rise before the throne of God (see, for example, Isaiah 2:2, 61:11, and 66:18). Already now we are seeing a supernatural multiplication of prayer rooms, cafés, warehouses, and commercial businesses all over the world playing "host" to the presence of God as they facilitate an atmosphere of unending worship and prayer.

This sound is being unleashed even from some of the most unlikely places on earth—such as a downtown skyscraper in China. During my last trip to China, we gathered hundreds of underground church worshipers in a downtown skyscraper for a 48-hour Burn of nonstop worship! The wealthy businessman who owned the entire complex (and several others) had always dreamed of seeing his business become a place where the sound of night-and-day worship could flow forth to bless the city. Our trip marked the official launch and dedication of the fifth floor of his skyscraper for the purpose of lavishing love and affection on Jesus. The building, located in the middle of the city's busy financial district, was the perfect, central location to host two days of unending worship.

Because the exploding underground house church movement in China is still under heavy persecution from the communist government, it is not safe for the church to hold large gatherings in public places. However, due to China's recent burst of economic growth and prosperity, incredible freedom has been granted to profit-producing businesses, and they experience little to no governmental interference. Therefore, this location provided the perfect safeguard for a gathering of believers from across China for a massive "bonfire" of worship.

The business owner allowed his employees to take one hour off in the middle of each workday to join in the worship on the fifth floor, realizing from previous worship ventures that there was a strong correlation between his business success and the hours of worship and prayer. The more they worshiped as a company, the higher their business profits soared! Hosting the presence of God—this could be a new model for businesses all over the world!

SPIRIT OF ENCOUNTER

Across planet earth, an entire generation is starving to know, feel, and experience the revelation of the beauty of Jesus. As it was with the persecutor Saul on the road to Damascus (see Acts 9) or Old Testament King Saul during his encounter with the singing minstrels (see 1 Sam. 10), everything changes during an encounter with His presence. Persecuting terrorists turn into healing revivalists, and evil kings turn into prophesying worshipers. All it takes is one divine and powerful encounter.

More than a tidy worship program consisting of three fast songs, three slow songs, a sonnet, and closing prayer, a spirit of encounter must mark our gatherings. This requires an entirely new definition of "seeker sensitive" church and "emerging" church. Here, the secret is not in watering down a service to make it more palatable to outsiders, but instead allowing the true seeker of hearts—the Holy Spirit—to take total control! The presence of God will speak for Himself when He invades our churches, cities, and regions and reveals the One whom all hearts long for. The Spirit's presence is not so fragile that He requires our help through lengthy explanations. We have seen the lost saved, the sick healed, and the saved revived without any preaching or altar call—the atmosphere of His presence is enough!

This means that a great responsibility falls on present-day worshipers to usher in this spirit of encounter. We have countless stories from around the world of hard-line Muslims in Iraq, prostitutes in Amsterdam, head witches in Salem, Massachusetts, and theology students at Harvard University having dramatic encounters leading to salvation, simply by stepping into the atmosphere of His presence. I believe that God is longing to release the spirit of encounter through worship in our day as never before, and we get to be His agents as we proclaim the truth of His glory, splendor, and fame everywhere we go.

REVELATION IN THE REPETITION

We recognize that we have encountered His presence when we catch a glimpse of the revelation of His beauty, majesty, and holiness. This revelation has captured the angels in their never-ending Revelation 4 chant, and this same revelation is what keeps us up throughout the night worshiping our hearts out before the Lord. We get a peek at the never-ending worship service in Heaven in the Book of Revelation. The heavenly beings have not yet moved on from their one-word wonder-song: "HOLY, HOLY, HOLY"! They have been singing it since the beginning of time and they do not seem inclined to change their words anytime soon.

This continuous vertical worship has to be more "caught" than it is taught. There is a special sound that releases a revelation of the distinct characteristics of God, and "catching" that sound does not require a Ph.D. in theology or even good music ability (although I'm not scoffing at those).

On a practical level, implementing simple yet repetitious phrases, verses, and chorus lines can help the assembled people to fully grasp the revelations that are coming forth spontaneously. For a long time church worship has been so regulated by hymnals or PowerPoint displays that we can fail to fulfill the direct command (repeated 87 times in the Bible) to "sing a new song to the Lord"!

Oftentimes, one-word songs will release new dimensions of the knowledge of God's glory that can be "caught" by over-churched believers as well as the under-churched and even the enemies of the faith.

The prophet Habakkuk declares: *"For the earth will be filled with the knowledge of the glory of the Lord as the waters cover the sea"* (Hab. 2:14). I believe this verse calls forth prophetically the day when worship will literally overrun the entire planet. Unless churches, cities, and nations hear and see the broadcasted revelation of the knowledge of God's beauty, holiness, and might, there is no hope for a turnaround. The activities of worship and cultivating a place of His presence are not just part of the heavenly strategy, but they simply represent *the* strategy for extending His Kingdom and dominion throughout the earth.

THE MUZZLE IS COMING OFF

Not long ago, I was leading worship for a large Sunday morning church service. The maximum-capacity attendance and multiple services that morning necessitated tight time restrictions in order to fit everything in. In my younger (and more unrefined) days, I would have been disturbed by the constraints, and I might have tried to press the envelope to extend the worship time. As you can imagine, this approach tends only to create tension, and it can come across as arrogant and dishonorable to the other leaders.

In this situation, I had already learned that God is not interested in empowering the ambition of independent renegades who disregard authority, although He longs to bring divine transformation through dependent sons and daughters. So I felt assured that the Holy Spirit could accomplish all He needed within our time constraints, and I was determined to stick to the planned order of service.

As I was leading the first song, the Lord downloaded to my spirit quite an unusual vision. I saw a very large and ferocious dog, like a K-9 police dog, with a muzzle firmly strapped around his mouth. The dog could not bark, bite, or attack because the muzzle was holding him back. The muzzle had domesticated and silenced him so that he could be treated more like a cute pet than a vicious dog. The Lord showed me that the dog represented the American Church, with its bark, bite, and attack against darkness all restrained due to a "muzzle of silence" over her. Because of this muzzle, the Church cannot operate in its intended function, and it ends up being viewed by the enemies of the Gospel as a mere cute pet.

Before leading into the next song, I explained the vision, and I prophesied that God longed to see the muzzle completely removed from His Church, in order to release the sound of worship and spiritual attack against darkness. I added a corporate prayer that God would "un-domesticate" our worship that morning. Needless to say, it was all over from there! The worship time literally took over the service in a new way that was so powerful it has yet to be repeated in my experience.

THE BUCKET LIST

As a 12-year-old, returning home from my very first mission trip with my dad to the remote jungles of the Amazon River, a fire burned in my heart. It had been a trip of many "firsts" for me: I had seen a demon shriek out of a person and a lame man walk for the first time in over 15 years after we laid hands on him. I had helped to baptize people in the Amazon River with piranhas swimming around my feet, and I had watched hearts melt at hearing the name "Jesus" for the first time. Now I did not want to go anywhere or do anything unless it involved the most unreached peoples of the world!

Back home, I hung a large map in my room that covered an entire wall, and I began to pray every night for the five most unreached nations on the planet. As I prayed, I asked God to give me the chance before I died to worship and share His love in each of those five nations. Needless to say, I was a pretty ambitious 12-year-old.

Fifteen years after those prayers began, I could boast of His faithfulness, because by then my feet had touched down in four out of five of those nations. This included two nations that were in the middle of war when we arrived (Afghanistan and Iraq). I have worshiped, preached, and almost gotten into a ton of trouble as I have witnessed the unstoppable move of God's presence invading each of those dark countries.

The open door for the nation ranking number one on my list swung open at the most unlikely of times. I was still grappling with the heartbreaking loss to cancer of my father six months earlier. Also, my wife had given birth three months earlier to a gorgeous, blonde, blue-eyed baby girl. We were now on the "beginner's ropes course" of parenting, and it did not seem like the best time for me to skip off to one of the most dangerous places on earth.

As I wrestled with whether or not to walk through this divine opportunity, the Spirit responded to the turmoil raging in my heart by saying, "Well, Sean, you are the one who asked for it!" With no excuses left, and with the blessing of my wife, I joined a small, fiery team a month later that was crazy enough to risk their lives to release the sound of Heaven in the darkest region of the world. Rated number one for the most severe Christian persecution by Voice of Martyrs and number one by the United Nations for the most closed and isolated people group in the world, I did not know of a single person who had stepped foot on the soil of that nation.

When our plane touched down on the tarmac at the Pyongyang airport in the capital city of North Korea, a song began to well up within my soul that I could not hold back. I had sneaked my guitar and Bible into the country, and I knew we would find it impossible to obey almost all of the rules our staunch military guides had given us (including, "don't sing," "don't pray," and "don't smile"). The song and melody that bubbled forth was truly like "rivers of living waters" overflowing from my belly—and it could potentially put us all into prison if I did not hold it back.

What surprised me is that the song coming forth was not a song of spiritual warfare, pain, sorrow, or heaviness! Most of the time, I feel I am a "contender" in worship, and I love singing songs to "rend the heavens" over dark nations in order to initiate spiritual breakthrough. I strongly believe in the role of aggressive worship in pushing back oppression and fear, because even Jesus declared, *the violent take it by force* (Matt. 11:12 NKJV). But what bubbled up in my spirit and came out of my mouth in the darkest, most closed nation on earth had nothing to do with this aggressive sound. The only kind of song I could sing for the entirety of our visit to North Korea was one of overwhelming joy!

The following verse became our theme as we traveled across North Korea.

> *Blessed is the people that know the joyful sound: they shall walk, O Lord, in the light of Thy countenance. In Thy name shall they rejoice all the day: and in Thy righteousness shall they be exalted. For Thou art the glory of their strength: and in Thy favour our horn shall be exalted* (Psalm 89:15-17 KJV).

Everywhere we went, we sang, we laughed, we prayed, and we smiled. We broke every rule and we had so much fun doing it! We released lightness wherever our feet stepped. As we sang, displacing heavy burdens with overwhelming joy and hope, an atmospheric shift took place. Even our AK-47-bearing military guides dropped their grimaces and began to ask us questions about the One about whom we were so happy! This spirit of "rejoicing all day long" opened doors for us that we could not have imagined beforehand.

On the last day of our trip, we were invited to visit the DMZ (Demilitarized Zone) between North and South Korea. For the past 50 years, this 180-mile-long border has been known as the most heavily fought-after piece of property on earth. More military weapons, ammunition, and armed soldiers are concentrated in this single area than anywhere else in the world. Since 1952, the two nations have been at war; and technically, they still are in a state of war.

A building straddles this treacherous border, built by the U.S. government in the 1970s to host peace and reunification talks between the enemy nations. From time to time, presidents, prime ministers, and foreign dignitaries have gathered with Korean leaders in the "blue room" (so dubbed because of its bright blue paint job) to see if they can make some progress toward this end.

When our team arrived in the DMZ, we could feel the weight of confusion, strife, and demonic tyranny in the environment. Having spent almost a week in the most oppressed, isolated, and persecuted nation on earth, now we were walking into the most heavily fought-after border territory as well. Talk about an intense atmosphere! None of us understood why they were bringing us here, as it is not a tourist-friendly sort of place, and it was definitely not on our original schedule.

Even though it was strictly forbidden, I had felt the Spirit's prompting to bring my guitar along. As we walked down through the endless ranks of North Korean infantry en route to a tour of the blue room, I began to feel strong stirrings of expectancy in my spirit—a divine setup from Heaven was well underway. I still do not even know to this day how God made my guitar "disappear" on the long walk down to the blue room. Although I tried my hardest to hide its bulkiness by walking with it behind my back, angels must have been standing around us to make it invisible to so many scrutinizing eyes.

Not that we ourselves were invisible. Our group of a few long-haired, white-skinned Americans (one of whom was trying to hide a guitar behind his back) was escorted by a regiment of armed North Korean soldiers in plain view of South Korean and American troops across the border! I did not know it was possible for human mouths to be held that wide open for such an extended amount of time! They stared and pointed their fingers in sheer disbelief at the sight they beheld.

ADD JOY TO THE CONTENTION

The moment we walked into the blue room, I felt the nudging of the Spirit to release the song of joy. Not only was this completely illegal (we had been warned not to talk, pray, and *definitely* not to sing), but added to that was the strong intimidation factor of over 30 armed North Korean soldiers in the room, all of whom seemed to be looking for an excuse to initiate combat! This wasn't quite a lively church crowd, for sure! I tried my best to ignore the Voice, which was quiet at first, and I resisted even more strenuously when it got louder and louder inside my spirit.

Finally, I could take it no more. I reached over to open my guitar case in the corner of the room. Again those angels must have shown up to make my guitar invisible to every soldier in there! Taking advantage of a small commotion made by some of my team members on the other end of the room (a brilliant distraction strategy), a song of joy began to flow effortlessly from my mouth and fingers. Immediately, I could feel a shift in the atmosphere of the place. The welcome presence of God invaded the stale, cold air. After the song had streamed forth for about five minutes, the invisible angels left me hanging, and the soldiers quickly shut down our worship session.

But the damage had already been done! The song of joy had been released from within the most contentious and fear-infested atmosphere on earth! We could almost feel the ground shift and the atmosphere shake. Once again, we knew that worship is taking over every crevice of our planet.

NO PLACE SAFE ANYMORE

Armed with testimonies from all over the world that are similar to this one, our global Burn 24-7 tribe has been boldly declaring everywhere God sends us that there is "no place safe anymore" from this sound of worship. It will infiltrate every dark and dictator-led country! It will flood the streets, ghettos, slums, mosques, and temples of the cities around the globe. It will even hijack our tidy Sunday morning church meetings! Like the sound of rushing waters, this sound of worship cannot be contained or controlled.

Even with the current explosion of houses of prayer, "furnaces of worship," and massive stadium worship gatherings, I do not believe we have seen anything yet. This is just the first few notes, the very beginning intro to the first verse of a fresh, abrasive, dynamic song of the Spirit that is rising in one generation. These early testimonies of breakthrough stir our hearts with hope for the fulfillment of Isaiah's words below:

> *For as the soil makes the sprout come up and a garden causes seeds to grow, so the Sovereign Lord will make righteousness and praise spring up before all nations* (Isaiah 61:11).

A GLOBAL TAKE-OVER

Ever since the humble and somewhat accidental beginnings of the Burn 24-7 movement on a college campus in a handful of burning hearts, God has expanded this move worldwide to places as unlikely as the blue room in the

Korean DMZ. Who knew that one breath of His Spirit on the glowing embers of our hearts during a midnight worship session in a stuffy dorm room could ignite an inferno that would spread like a wildfire all over the world! Our humble testimony of being "caught up" in this move is evidence enough of its scope and power.

As you are reading this today, the downtown flats of Minneapolis, Native American reservations across South Dakota, Hindu temples throughout India, makeshift tents perched in earthquake-wracked Haiti, doorways in the red-light district in Amsterdam, underground basements in Iran, and jungle huts of Indonesia are now burning with a fire of worship that will not be extinguished. This fire has ushered in waves of healings and salvations across these regions, as only the presence of God can, shifting entire regions into Kingdom breakthrough.

We will see things that are even more outrageous than worship in a downtown skyscraper in communist China. According to God's promise, a new breed of worshiping missionaries (or "musicianaries" as we call them), armed with this sound and reality of His overshadowing presence, will unleash His glory into the darkness where He has not been known and where He has been despised. These troubadours of worship are the Zinzendorfs of a new day, and they will not stop or shut up until every molecule of this planet joins in the Revelation song of the Lamb.

From our Fire and Fragrance training schools (partnering with YWAM, the largest mission movement in modern history) to our Burning Ones internships, to our many leadership summits, short- and long-term mission teams, conferences, and roundtables held all over the world, Burn 24-7 is bent on calling forth and sending out an influx of present-day psalmists and worshipers to the four corners of the earth! As more and more burning hearts join in the greatest heist of the planet in the history of the world, praise and worship will spring forth from every nation, tribe, and tongue. Such continual, all-encompassing worship will bring forth a complete atmospheric shift from darkness, oppression, and hopelessness to light, joy, and peace, preparing the way for Jesus' return to earth!

REJOICE

(© Sean Feucht)

Rejoice, you desert, rejoice
Let the parched land be glad.
For here come the flowing springs,
Carrying the joy that you need.
Strengthen all the feeble hands
And the knees that give way,
For He has not forgotten you.
Here He comes, bringing the new!
Rejoice, O rejoice!
Lift up your voices and make a noise.
Rejoice, O rejoice!
Winter is gone and the spring has come
Sing, O barren woman, you who have no child,
For greater will be your offspring
Than those who have it all.
Make way, you wilderness,
Prepare to burst into bloom.
The lame will leap like a deer;
The mute tongue will open and sing.

Chapter Six

WORSHIP PRECEDES THE PRESENCE

JAMES W. GOLL

Worship and prayer form the seamless garment the priest wears as he ministers unto the Lord. Where does worship end and prayer begin? In my experience, they just ebb and flow together like the tides of the ocean, supernaturally-naturally. In the ministry of the priesthood of all believers, I see no clear demarcation between something called "worship" and something called "prayer."

You were born to worship God now and throughout all eternity. What a job description! After you "enter in," you are then empowered to be a deliverer of others. Worship and prayer are not ends in themselves; they lead to the very presence of God Himself.

A HISTORIC CASE STUDY

It was 1949. The two elderly sisters were desperate. Peggy and Christine Smith, at 82 and 84 years of age, were too frail to leave their cottage in the village of Barvas on the island of Lewis in the Hebrides islands off Scotland, but they wanted more than anything to see revival on their island.

So they decided to undertake a prayer campaign together. Twice a week, the two old women got on their knees at ten o'clock in the late evening, and they prayed until at least three or four o'clock in the morning. In particular, they prayed (in their native Gaelic) from the words of Isaiah 64:1: "Lord, 'rend the heavens and come down'!" They claimed the promises of another passage from the Book of Isaiah, repeatedly:

> For I will pour water upon him that is thirsty, and floods upon the dry ground: I will pour My spirit upon thy seed, and My blessing upon thine offspring: And they shall spring up as among the grass, as willows by the water courses (Isaiah 44:3-4 KJV).

Although Peggy was blind and Christine was crippled with arthritis, they kept praying like this for weeks.

While they were praying, a group of seven young men who were office-holders in the local parish began to pray for revival as well. They met in an unheated barn for their prayer meetings on Tuesday and Friday nights. Sometimes they got so cold they had to crawl into the haystacks in order to keep warm. One night, one of the deacons stood up and read from the Book of Psalms:

> Who shall ascend into the hill of the Lord? or who shall stand in His holy place? He that hath clean hands, and a pure heart; who hath not lifted up his soul unto vanity, nor sworn deceitfully. He shall receive the blessing from the Lord, and righteousness from the God of his salvation (Psalm 24:3-5 KJV).

Purity! Without "clean hands and a pure heart," nobody could expect a true visitation from God.

One night in the cottage, Peggy (the one who was blind!) received a vision. She saw the church filled with young people—and up until that time, none of the young people of the village were attending the church—and she started proclaiming, "He is coming! He is coming! He's already here!" She told her younger sister to go tell their pastor that God wanted him to find an evangelist and bring him to speak at the village church.

The pastor inquired around, and he found a young evangelist named Duncan Campbell who was willing to come and preach. Campbell responded only because the pastor persisted. He had other speaking engagements and he felt he could not do it. But when those other engagements were inexplicably canceled, he accepted.

Late at night, at the end of Campbell's first service, something unprecedented happened. Outside the doors of the church, a crowd of 600 villagers gathered spontaneously. About a hundred of them were young people who had been at a dance in the parish hall. They had just "fled from the hall as a man fleeing from a plague," according to Campbell's later account, and had come to the church because the lights were on. People who had already gone to bed had gotten up, put their clothes back on, and walked out into the night toward the church as well.[1]

Campbell had agreed to a ten-day engagement, but the first wave of revival lasted five weeks. Day and night, worship services and prayer meetings were held. After a brief lull, the revival resumed. Young and old came to faith in Jesus, including even the most inveterate sinners. Something like a "spiritual radiation zone" was reported to have surrounded the church, and people who entered that zone were never the same. Many of them were seized with a conviction of their sin and saved by the sovereign power of God's presence even before they heard Campbell's preaching.

Because of the sacrificial prayers of a handful of faithful worshipers, almost every person on the island had encountered the living God. Campbell is the one who has gone down in the history books as the one who ushered in the Hebrides revival, but the credit should go to the two old women and seven young men from the village whose worship and intercession opened the way for the visitation of God. Without their earnest, expectant prayers and worship, the presence of God may never have been powerful enough to be noticed.

At least one disciple (or, better, more than one person) needed to have offered an extended sacrifice of worshipful prayer, allowing His Spirit to sweep everything clean, and inviting God to come and take up residence.

NEEDED: MINISTRY AT THE ALTAR OF INCENSE

Any of us can enter into the ministry of worship and prayer. Those nine Scots were just ordinary Christians whose passion for God matched their desire to follow the leading of the Holy Spirit. Their sacrifice released a power from on high that altered church history. Any of us can do the same.

I did not begin as an intercessor. I began by singing the praises of God in my youth. At times, I served as the altar boy, lighting the candles before the worship service. To be honest, that job was a real sacrifice. I really did not like putting on that silly robe. But the task that was not a sacrifice for me in the least, but rather a true delight, was when I was asked to climb up into the balcony overlooking the sanctuary, and I would begin the entire worship service by singing the prelude. From my perch in the loft, I would sing out, *a cappella*, "The Lord is in His holy temple. Let all the earth keep silence before Him." Oh, how I loved my perch!

You see, in traditional church liturgy, worship is supposed to precede the Word and His Word precedes His presence. Yet, we need a revelation in our day that goes beyond Christian tradition, reaching back to the ancient altar of incense.

It is happening. So much change has occurred. We are living in the midst of the greatest global worship and prayer movement the Church has ever witnessed. And it is growing. Around the world, centers for 24/7/365 prayer are emerging.

This is a great improvement from how it used to be, when only a handful of "prayer specialists" could stand before God on behalf of the people. In the

Old Testament, right up to the time of Jesus, only the priests—often only one particular one, who had been chosen by lot—could represent the needs of the people before God. Within the tabernacle of Moses, the altar of incense was the fifth station where the priests would minister, and it stood right in front of the most holy place. As the worship of the nation of Israel developed over the centuries, individual priests would be selected by lot to burn incense there.

These days, we often interpret incense to mean the prayers of the saints. In fact, because of Paul's statement, *"you also, as living stones, are being built up a spiritual house, a holy priesthood, to offer up spiritual sacrifices acceptable to God through Jesus Christ"* (1 Pet. 2:5 NKJV), we know that any one of us can, in essence, pray at the altar of incense. It is the right and privilege of every priest, and now all of us are priests in God's house. You may have noticed that the New Testament does not include "worship" or "prayer" in its lists of special spiritual gifts. That is because it is the calling of each and every one of us.

In the year before Jesus was born, his uncle Zechariah who was a priest, got chosen by lot to be the priest who would get to burn incense before the Holy of Holies. (See Luke 1:8-11.) Zechariah and his wife, Elizabeth, were both *"very old"* (Luke 1:7). He had waited all his priestly life for this. As far as we know, this was the first time he had been chosen to burn incense. The smoke of the incense (and prayers) would go up to Heaven and, unless some spiritual interference was encountered, the presence of God would come down. It is like Holy Ghost gravity; what goes up, must come down.

With the entire congregation standing in prayer outside, he went in. His role was to stand in for the people, before God. He wasn't thinking of himself, only of reaching God on behalf of the people. I would call that "pure worship."

Suddenly and without any warning, an angel accosted him:

> *Then an angel of the Lord appeared to him, standing at the right side of the altar of incense. When Zechariah saw him, he was startled and was gripped with fear. But the angel said to him:*

"Do not be afraid, Zechariah; your prayer has been heard. Your wife Elizabeth will bear you a son, and you are to call him John" (Luke 1:11-13).

Prayer and incense rose up to Heaven. The presence of God came down. Zechariah went home to Elizabeth, stricken mute because of what had happened, and he was able to explain a little of what had happened by means of a writing tablet. Before long, Elizabeth's lifelong barrenness—which was all the more distressing because in that culture fertility was considered a sign of God's blessing, and because of the fact that she was now too old to bear a child—was reversed. She got pregnant, and she bore a son whom they named John, after which Zechariah could speak again.

Who was this son John? He grew up to become John the Baptist. God's presence had worked miracle on top of miracle, initiated by Zechariah's prayer at the altar of incense.

As I look around today, I see and hear fresh prayers going up like incense to God. "More, Lord!" is the cry. A transgenerational anointing has mobilized young people as well as seasoned saints to worship their hearts out, expectantly. Once again, prayer, worship, and intercession are rising up and creating an opening for the manifest presence of God.

KEYS TO UNLOCK HEAVEN

Another way of saying it would be to call prayerful worship one of the primary *keys* that opens the way to God's glorious presence. Sustained, pure worship is one key that always opens the gates of Heaven.

A second key is prophetic revelation. As we saw with Peggy Smith, wonderful visions and words from God can come forth when a truly desperate person becomes convinced that God alone is the answer and seeks Him relentlessly. Personal brokenness is a good part of it.

Worshipers who cannot stop seeking His face know the truth of Jesus' words: *"It is written: 'Man shall not live on bread alone, but on every word that comes from the mouth of God'"* (Matt. 4:4. Jesus was quoting Deuteronomy 8:3).

Revelation means getting words from God—*living* words, words that are actively "proceeding" from His mouth. And when we seek God, get a living (*rhema*) word from Him, and then put that revelatory key word into our prayers, His presence will come rushing in. We pray His words back to Him. We know we are praying according to His will, because He just told us what He wants. Without fail, He will show up.

The Word of God is also referred to in the Bible as a sword: *"...the sword of the Spirit, which is the word of God"* (Eph. 6:17). Words that have come straight from God are effective against impossible odds. These are not the same as rote, systematized words that may at one time have borne a divine touch but that carry hardly a trace of it anymore. We have all tried to do it, but we should know by now that we cannot turn what God said yesterday into a lucky rabbit's foot for today.

As we have been learning throughout this book, God is relational. With Him, your worship is personal. Before Him, you are ever so aware of your dependency upon Him. When you worship before Him and He gives you a word, His Spirit will show you what to do with it. It is the best methodology I know for bringing in the Kingdom of God.

BREAK OPEN THE WAY

Spiritual principles stand firm always, but we are not worshiping spiritual principles. It is easy to fall into doing just that. "If you worship this way, ABC, God will show up this way, XYZ." That is not a relationship; it is a system, a performance- and equation-oriented system.

Instead of following established systems, we need to follow our pioneer Himself, Jesus, who broke open the way to God the Father. He had a few choice words for the religious experts whose legalism keeps people from doing this:

> *Woe to you experts in the law, because you have taken away the key to knowledge. You yourselves have not entered, and you have hindered those who were entering* (Luke 11:52).

Too often, invested authorities hold on too tightly to the keys that have been delegated to them. Instead of using the revelatory key to open closed minds, closed doors, and closed situations, they prefer to use it to fortify their own "control spirit," which turns out to be a definite hindrance to welcoming the Spirit of the living God.

Can we wiggle free of such control and create an atmosphere where God will be welcome? Yes, if we want to do it. We can become "breakers," who, following a lifestyle of pure, sacrificial worship, can pass through gates that were formerly closed and can break open a way on behalf of others: *"The breaker goes up before them; they break out, pass through the gate and go out by it. So their king goes on before them, and the Lord at their head"* (Mic. 2:13 NASB).

Now, we must recognize the fact that breakers must first be broken. Like Jesus, who is the ultimate broken breaker, ardent worshipers whose greatest desire is to see God's Kingdom come in greater measure must worship Him as humble, needy, and transparent people. They must love others and the very place of the community with God's own heart of love. They are not seeking "salvation notches" on their belts when they weep over their cities as Jesus wept over Jerusalem.

These people are pioneer point people. Their prayers and worship can help break open the way like Holy Spirit bulldozers, pushing the debris out of God's way. Sometimes when they are deep in prayer (and this happened with the people who prayed in the revival in the Hebrides), they feel like women in travail at childbirth. This makes sense, because their prayers are widening and opening the "birth canal" so that a new life, conceived in intimacy, can come forth.

Breakers can break open the gates of the enemy, as well, taking back what he has stolen and creating more breathing room for the Spirit.

Their brokenness in worship leads to purity, clarity, and openness, as portrayed by Isaiah:

> *Pass through, pass through the gates! Prepare the way for the people. Build up, build up the highway! Remove the stones. Raise a banner for the nations. The Lord has made proclamation to the ends of the earth: "Say to Daughter Zion, 'See, your Savior comes! See, His reward is with Him, and His recompense accompanies Him.'" They will be called the Holy People, the Redeemed of the Lord; and you will be called Sought After, the City No Longer Deserted* (Isaiah 62:10-12).

This is the ultimate goal of pure worship. Having proceeded to the Father through Jesus Christ, worship becomes a weapon of spiritual warfare and a tool for building a highway upon which the Lord Himself may come, revealing Himself and redeeming a people for His Kingdom. God's supreme purpose is to restore all of His creation.

OPENING GATES AND DOORS

Right after I moved to the greater Nashville area from Kansas City, I spent a solid year studying gates and doors. I read about gates and doors in the Bible; I read about them in history; I read about them in the context of various Middle Eastern cultures. After all that reading and rumination, I came to a ridiculously simple conclusion: Gates and doors are closed to shut things out, and they are opened to let things in.

God gives keys for opening doors, and He has gatekeepers. Who are the gatekeepers? Those who spend time by the gates, in particular the gates that lead to Heaven. Having the ability to shut the demonic gates behind them, they maintain consistent attitudes of thanksgiving, praise, and sacrifice so that the gates to Heaven will fly open before them and they can lead others through in triumph:

> *Enter into His gates with thanksgiving, and into His courts with praise. Be thankful to Him, and bless His name* (Psalm 100:4 NKJV).

We worshipers have been called to possess the gates. We have been invested with the authority to claim the inheritance of what Jesus Christ has redeemed for us. We have the ability, because of His Spirit, to take back the gates that have been stolen by enemy forces, and to overcome all opposition. We walk in the footsteps of Peter, to whom Jesus said, *"And I also say to you that you are Peter, and on this rock I will build My church, and the gates of Hades shall not prevail against it"* (Matt. 16:18 NKJV).

This has been true for centuries, and it is true for us because we are of the "seed" of Abraham, and it has always been part of the Master Plan:

> *"...indeed I will greatly bless you, and I will greatly multiply your seed as the stars of the heavens and as the sand which is on the seashore; and your seed shall possess the gate of their enemies. In your seed all the nations of the earth shall be blessed, because you have obeyed My voice"* (Genesis 22:17-18 NASB).

Here God prophesied to Abraham that through his seed (which Galatians 3:16 indicates is Christ), all the nations of the earth would be blessed. How would this be accomplished? By those of us who are one with Christ and with His purposes. When we so wholly align ourselves with Him that we can repossess the gates with Him, once again they can be shut against evil and opened to the dawning light of the new day.

Am I on a rabbit trail here? Not at all. What does all this have to do with pure worship? Everything!

The only way to go through a gate, biblically, is with pure worship. Do you remember what the Scottish deacon in the haystack read aloud in the story at the beginning of this chapter? Here it is again, in the ringing words of the King James version:

> *Who shall ascend into the hill of the Lord? or who shall stand in His holy place? He that hath clean hands, and a pure heart; who hath not lifted up his soul unto vanity, nor sworn deceitfully. He shall receive the blessing from the Lord, and righteousness from the God of his salvation* (Psalm 24:3-5 KJV).

This is both a Messianic prophecy concerning the historic moment when the King of Glory (Jesus Christ) would take the "keys" and repossess Heaven, and it is also a prophetic declaration about how seamless prayer and worship opens the way from Heaven to earth, so that the power and glory of God's presence can be released into our midst and come to our aid.

I am convinced that the collected Church within specific geographical areas needs to shoulder its responsibility as the gatekeeper. Together with the marketplace leaders (who are like the business people in Bible times who conducted their transactions within the shadow of the immense city gates), the gatekeepers know who to let in and who to forbid. In a very real way, the worshiping people of God stand in for Jesus Himself. Jesus needs to be honored as the chief Gatekeeper, because that is how He portrayed Himself:

> *Therefore Jesus said again, "Very truly I tell you, I am the gate for the sheep. All who have come before Me are thieves and robbers, but the sheep have not listened to them. I am the gate; whoever enters through Me will be saved. They will come in and go out, and find pasture* (John 10:7-9).

ENTERING INTO HIS PRESENCE

How can the people of God open His gates? By now, the answer to that question should have become a review. We enter His gates with *thanksgiving* (see Ps. 100:4), and with *praise* (see Isa. 60:18b). When we *worship* together, we can march forward in *unity,* and our feet can stand strong regardless of the circumstances. (See Hebrews 12:28 and Psalm 133:1.) As long as we move forward in His strength, and not our own puny facsimile of strength, He will be sure to open every gate and engulf us in the light of His manifest presence (see Ps. 51:17).

The people of God may come from every tribe and nation. They represent every generation and every economic class. They don't dress the same and they don't speak the same languages. They do not beat their drums the same or dance the same. The only thing that unifies them and that distinguishes them from the rest of the people on the planet is God's presence. His Spirit dwells within them individually and corporately.

Our ongoing worship for Him ensures His ongoing presence with us. We value that, even more than Moses did when he had this conversation with the Lord God:

> *"If You are pleased with me, teach me Your ways so I may know You and continue to find favor with You. Remember that this nation is Your people."*
>
> *The Lord replied, "My Presence will go with you, and I will give you rest."*
>
> *Then Moses said to Him, "If Your Presence does not go with us, do not send us up from here. How will anyone know that You are pleased with me and with Your people unless You go with us? What else will distinguish me and Your people from all the other people on the face of the earth?"*
>
> *And the Lord said to Moses, "I will do the very thing you have asked, because I am pleased with you and I know you by name."*
>
> *Then Moses said, "Now show me Your glory"* (Exodus 33:13-18).

Moses' God is our God, and He wants us to release His brilliant, glorious presence wherever we go. He is the same yesterday, today, and forever (see Heb. 13:8). Once you have tasted of the goodness of His presence, nothing else will satisfy you. Even one day of His presence is better than the best the world could ever offer you.

Enter His gates with thanksgiving and praise. Worship your way in. Because...

Better is one day in Your courts than a thousand elsewhere; I would rather be a doorkeeper in the house of my God than dwell in the tents of the wicked. For the Lord God is a sun and shield; the Lord bestows favor and honor; no good thing does He withhold from those whose walk is blameless. Lord Almighty, blessed is the one who trusts in You (Psalm 84:10-12).

As for me and my house, at the end of the day, we will be worshipers of the Lord. We will lift up holy hands to the One who is worthy. We will minister to the Lord, and bless His holy name. And as we worship the King, He will pour out the abundance of the reign of His presence upon us. We hope to see the latter rain of His presence flood the earth as the waters cover the seas.

O WORSHIP THE KING

(by Robert Grant, public domain)

O worship the King, all glorious above,
O gratefully sing His power and His love;
Our Shield and Defender, the Ancient of Days,
Pavilioned in splendor, and girded with praise.

O tell of His might, O sing of His grace,
Whose robe is the light, whose canopy space,
His chariots of wrath the deep thunderclouds form,
And dark is His path on the wings of the storm.

The earth with its store of wonders untold,
Almighty, Thy power hath founded of old;
Established it fast by a changeless decree,
And round it hath cast, like a mantle, the sea.

Frail children of dust, and feeble as frail,
In Thee do we trust, nor find Thee to fail;
Thy mercies how tender, how firm to the end,
Our Maker, Defender, Redeemer, and Friend.

ENDNOTE

1. The story of the Hebrides Revival has been widely published. Many of these details come from an account by Duncan Campbell entitled "Revival in the Hebrides (1949)" (1968), transcript available at Shilohouse Ministries, http://www.shilohouse.org/Hebrides_Revival.htm, and from "When the Mountains Flowed Down," an article adapted from a taped message delivered by Duncan Campbell to the students of the Faith Mission Bible College in Edinburgh, Scotland. It chronicles some of Campbell's experiences and insights related to the Hebrides revival from 1949–1953 and is archived online at http://www.openheaven.com/library/history/lewis.html.

Chapter Seven

THE AUTHENTIC WORSHIPER

JEFF DEYO

By the grace of God, I have enjoyed many incredible privileges and blessings in my life and ministry. I have led worship around the globe, sometimes before crowds of tens of thousands in stadiums and outdoor festivals, and other times in small meetings in high school gymnasiums and various home prayer gatherings. I was the lead singer in an internationally known, Dove award-winning, Grammy-nominated worship band, and have had the opportunity to produce some influential CDs. Many of my songs are original compositions, but I am also known for my unique up-tempo arrangements of other people's music. But none of this is what is ultimately important to me. I live to worship. Worship oozes out of my soul. Worship is who I am, not just what I sing. It is the one thing I can offer in this life that is eternal in nature.

If I could sum up my private life and my public ministry in one word, it would be *authenticity*. After years of receiving heartfelt appreciation from concert-goers and fellow worshipers regarding what comes across to them as authentic ministry, I have truly begun to understand how important this characteristic is to people. There is no doubt that this concept has become a deeply foundational and scriptural one for me as I continue to grow as a Kingdom worshiper, a disciple of Christ, and a true Jesus-follower. Truly living, off the stage, as the person that people believe I am as a leader on the stage, has become one of the most important things in my life.

In First Timothy and Titus, Paul speaks about what is expected of elders, or any godly leaders—that they are to be held to a higher standard. The same is true for all Christians, because of the "Kingdom of priests" covenant (see 1 Pet. 2:9). God holds all of us to a high standard, simply because we possess the power of the Spirit. Therefore, we need to move from "practicing what we preach" to "preaching what we practice."

Notice how often hype, fakery, and human charisma pass for worship in what we might call "professional" church services. "God bless you" and "Hallelujah" often get used as transitional statements between songs and segments of the service rather than as genuine offerings of praise. Close your eyes; can't you hear it? That hyped-up preacher voice following a power-packed praise chorus with, "Halleluuuuu-jah, praise the Lord! Lift up a clap offering unto the Lord! Welcome saints to the house of Almighty God this glorious Sunday morning. Can't you just feel His magnificent presence in this place? God is good...all the time!"

Now these same phrases could absolutely be said with conviction and authenticity. It's just that so many times they're not. Why does this occur so often? What happens to normal people when they step onto a religious platform? All these religious phrases come flying out of their mouths, with religious gestures to match. Instead of simply being themselves, people transform into someone who comes across pompous, scripted, and fake, seemingly void of the Spirit.

I just couldn't live with myself knowing I'm acting like a true worshiper on the stage when I am really not a true worshiper off the stage. I couldn't get up there to lead people to magnify God's name when all the while I know in my heart that my relationship with God is virtually non-existent.

MINDLESS OFFERINGS

The writer of Ecclesiastes refers to this when it says, *"As you enter the house of God, keep your ears open and your mouth shut! Don't be a fool who doesn't realize that mindless offerings to God are evil"* (Eccles. 5:1 NLT).

You might not have thought of it this way, but the third commandment also highlights this idea: *"Do not misuse the name of the Lord your God. The Lord will not let you go unpunished if you misuse His name"* (Deut. 5:11 NLT). We have grown up understanding that we are not supposed to take the Lord's name in vain, but we view this only as it pertains to not using His name as a curse word. But cursing with the Lord's name is only one form of this. What if we use His name or speak of Him as Misty Edwards says in her song, "Dove's Eyes," "... like He's not in the room"—using His name and praising Him for no heartfelt purpose, for a filler, to woo the crowd, to build the moment—instead of in real relationship?

When we say, "Praise the Lord" and we don't mean it, that's not only *similar* to using the Lord's name in vain; it *is* using the Lord's name in vain.

Of course I do not mean we should stop saying "praise the Lord" altogether. That would be throwing out the baby with the bathwater. But clearly we need to stop going through the motions, "doing church"—as if it is a formula, a strategy, a business. If we are not careful, we can end up manufacturing a false God-encounter in our services, laden with hype and religious lingo but without true relationship.

I do not want to be a part of a church machine, and I know you don't, either. Worship is supposed to be a living, breathing, supernatural encounter with God that has been founded on Christ and constructed from living human stones that are united as a body to form the structure of the temple of God.

BONA FIDE CHRIST-FOLLOWERS

You Samaritans know so little about the one you worship, while we Jews know all about Him, for salvation comes through the Jews. But the time is coming and is already here when true worshipers will worship the Father in spirit and in truth. The Father is looking for anyone who will worship Him that way. For God is Spirit, so those who worship Him must worship in spirit and in truth (John 4:22-24 NLT).

These lines from the story of Jesus talking with the woman at the well have to do with worship, and I want to highlight the message of authenticity found here. Jesus tells the woman (and by extension, all of us) that the Father is looking for, or seeking, true worshipers. I do not find it trivial that the four-letter word *true* appears right before the word *worshipers*. It would not be there if Jesus did not find it to be absolutely necessary.

Among other things, using the word *true* reveals to us that false worshipers do exist. By this I do not mean the obvious false worshipers of Baal, Buddha, Athena, or Allah. I am referring to people right in our own churches who have become false worshipers without even knowing it—people who stand next to us singing worship songs with hands lifted high, who attend a weekly life group, and who take communion alongside everyone else. Some of these people may even be pastors, worship leaders, or church staff members.

These folks may be worshiping the songs or the music instead of the One who created music, exalting the pastor instead of the One who fashioned and called him, adoring the feel-good experience of being part of a church community of passionate people instead of Christ Himself, the head of the Church.

God is looking for true worshipers. He is not looking for church-goers. He is looking for true disciples. He is not looking for bandwagon-jumpers. He is looking for passionate, Kingdom warriors who will honor Him with their songs, their decisions, their money, their time, their talents, their voices, and their lives!

The word *worshiper* could easily be replaced with the words *disciple* or *servant* or the phrases *Christ-follower* or *friend of God*. God is looking for true disciples, and a true disciple is the same as a true worshiper. The worshipers Jesus refers to are not specifically singers. We must remember that worship has only some part to do with music. In his book, *God Songs*, Paul Baloche wrote, "Worship is not music. But worship can be music."[1] When we worship God, we do so with our lives (our thoughts, speech, and actions), not only with our lips. In fact, our lives speak infinitely louder than the songs we sing.

The first time I read the phrase in John 4:23, "The Father is looking for anyone who will worship Him that way," I slammed on the brakes. To some people, it may not look like a very exciting sentence, but if you look again, you will realize it answers one of life's deepest questions: "God, what do You want from me?" Out of all the many, many things God could be looking for, He says here that He is looking for true worshipers. Think about that. This may or may not be *the* most important thing God wants to see, but it is definitely *one* of the things He highlights. And that is why I have underlined, circled, and starred this passage in my Bible. God is looking for true worshipers. Authentic followers of Christ. Real Christians. Genuine God-chasers. Unadulterated disciples. Bona fide believers. He is searching for people who will follow Him without reserve, with utter dependence, with complete surrender.

God is wondering if any of the readers of this book are true worshipers. He is wondering if the writers of this book will actually live what they write.

Lots of people go to church, but are they true worshipers? Are you? Am I? Is anyone on the earth a true worshiper? Since false worshipers do exist, could I not be one of them, even while believing I am a true worshiper? Could I not be singing the songs or even writing this chapter, all the while being deceived? It is sobering, isn't it?

Look at what Second Timothy 3:13 says: *"But evil people and impostors will flourish. They will deceive others and will themselves be deceived"* (NLT).

Hebrews 3:13 agrees: *"You must warn each other every day, while it is still 'today,' so that none of you will be deceived by sin and hardened against God"* (NLT). So without worrying about others, let us first ask ourselves the question, "Am I a true worshiper?"

MUSIC TO HIS EARS

People who want to understand worship often turn to the Book of Psalms to find relevant truth. But Psalms is not the only place in the Bible to find truths about music. Take Amos 5:21-24, for instance. Speaking for God as His prophet, Amos was not afraid to tell it like it is:

> *I hate all your show and pretense—the hypocrisy of your religious festivals and solemn assemblies. I will not accept your burnt offerings and grain offerings. I won't even notice all your choice peace offerings. Away with your noisy hymns of praise! I will not listen to the music of your harps. Instead, I want to see a mighty flood of justice, an endless river of righteous living* (Amos 5:21-24 NLT).

"I hate all your show and pretense...." God *hates*? Yes. He hates things that destroy His people. And He knows that show and pretense will destroy His people. That means He hates to see people pretending to be something they are not, behaving in an inauthentic way. In our lives, He hates hype and fake passion. In our worship, these things are noise to His ears (see verse 23).

Each version of the Bible brings out different aspects. You and I may not find "religious festivals and solemn assemblies" to be relevant, but look how *The Message* puts it:

> *I can't stand your religious meetings. I'm fed up with your conferences and conventions. I want nothing to do with your religion projects, your pretentious slogans and goals. I'm sick of your fund-raising schemes, your public relations and image making.*

I've had all I can take of your noisy ego-music. When was the last time you sang to Me? Do you know what I want? I want justice—oceans of it. I want fairness—rivers of it. That's what I want. That's all I want (Amos 5:21-24 TM).

It's not that God hates music or church services or conferences. It's that He is looking past the sound and the lights. He is looking into the hearts of each person present.

Maybe we have been missing the point all along. Maybe the things we have emphasized in church are not the things God is looking for after all. Maybe when God said turn left, we turned right and completely missed His heart on the matter. What is His heart on the matter? He tells us He does not like anything void of the authenticity and purity of the Kingdom. He hates lip service. He hates to see us going through religious motions and escapades while we are not even loving each other.

He wants "justice" more than He wants mellifluous harmonies. (And by the way, "justice" should not be solely defined as social justice, though this is important too.) He wants righteousness more than off-the-chart drum fills, vocal licks, or guitar solos.

Some of us like black gospel. Some like country. Some like hardcore or emo. Some like pop, and some like classical. When you hear a particular style of music, it makes you want to turn up (or down) the volume. God's musical tastes, however, have very little to do with style.

You might ask, "Then what is music to God's ears?" According to Amos' prophecy, it is righteousness (right living) and justice (lawfulness, just conduct, moral rightness). Of course He loves to hear His people take the gift of music and make it soar—but only when their worship is coming straight from righteous hearts. God "turns up the volume" when our offerings of praise are yoked to true, authentic justice and righteous living.

Obedience is music to God's ears—doing what He asks us to do even when nobody else is doing it. Music to God's ears is taking care of those who can't take care of themselves. Music to God's ears is setting the captives free, feeding the hungry, loving your husband or wife, blessing your employees, taking time for your kids, comforting the brokenhearted, helping the afflicted, healing the blind, and giving a cup of cold water to the thirsty. Music to God's ears is integrity, honesty, purity, loyalty, kindness, and faithfulness. Music to God's ears is James 1:27—taking care of orphans and widows *and* remaining uncorrupted by the world. Music to God's ears is much, much more than a song.

YOUR LIFE IS A SONG

To God, your whole life is like a song. To Him, each thing you do on this earth is like a note on a musical staff, and He's listening for the melody and harmony. What does your life sound like to Him? If you were to back up all the way to the day of your birth and view every action, thought, and word as a note in a cumulative orchestration, what would it sound like?

I imagine most of us would have measures in our songs where the music sounds dark and dissonant. We might find some odd time signatures or some times when everything is completely off-kilter. We would come across atonal sections and other parts that are just completely chaotic. In all likelihood, there would be random tempos, inappropriate dynamics, arbitrary melodies, missing sections, and plain old sour notes. The whole thing might be entirely out of key, or include a few awkward bars that sound as if someone suddenly slammed both hands down on a keyboard. Of course, parts of it would sound sweet and wonderful, too. But without a doubt, you and I would be mortified to have our true life song played before an audience.

Regardless of how our life songs have played out up to this point, we have a Savior, and He has swept in to begin helping us to rewrite our song. From this day forward, until we take our final breath, we can participate in creating a new song, a supernatural song, a God song. Because of Jesus, our previous life song does not have to be included in the repertoire. And that is good news.

THE SOUND OF OBEDIENCE

Jesus said, *"Not all people who sound religious are really godly. They may refer to Me as 'Lord,' but they still won't enter the Kingdom of Heaven. The decisive issue is whether they obey My Father in heaven"* (Matt. 7:21 NLT).

As a musician, I love this verse because it is real and in your face, and also because it uses the word *sound*. We are surrounded by so much sound in our lives: radios, TVs, DVDs, iPods, MP3s, concerts, singing, music. Our churches surround us with the sounds of worship, preaching, teaching, choirs, bands, organs, drums, prophecy, speaking in tongues, altar music. It may all sound religious to us, but God hears things differently. To Him, if a sound has not come from an obedient heart, that sound is not godly. It's not that people have to be perfect to do music, but once again we have to remember that the sound of our lives greatly overshadows the sound of our music.

It does not matter who they are—worship leaders, pastors. Jesus continues:

On judgment day many will tell Me, "Lord, Lord, we prophesied in Your name and cast out demons in Your name and performed many miracles in Your name." But I will reply, "I never knew you. Go away; the things you did were unauthorized."

Anyone who listens to My teaching and obeys Me is wise, like a person who builds a house on solid rock. Though the rain comes in torrents and the floodwaters rise and the winds beat against that house, it won't collapse, because it is built on rock. But anyone who hears My teaching and ignores it is foolish, like a person who builds a house on sand. When the rains and floods come and the winds beat against that house, it will fall with a mighty crash (Matthew 7:22-27 NLT).

This is a serious word, isn't it? As convicting as it may be, it comes with more than a dire diagnosis of our condition. It offers a glimmer of hope—it is never too late to begin obeying God. "The decisive issue is whether they obey My

Father in Heaven." It all starts with obedience. And *that* is beautiful music to God's ears. *"Those who obey My commandments are the ones who love Me"* (John 14:21 NLT). I suppose you could say it is really all about love; and love is all about obedience, which is all about trust and dying to self, which is an exquisite act of worship to our God.

The good news is we *can* obey, by means of the unstoppable power of God alive in us. As we worship through obedience and lay our lives down before Him, we will become more and more authentic. Then we will be truly authentic worshipers, the ones whose lips no longer discharge meaningless religious verbiage, but ones whose hearts and lives are in complete agreement with what we are singing and saying. Instead of putting our energy into looking good on the outside, we will develop the hidden areas of our lives, obeying everything He asks of us. We will spend time with Him when nobody is watching and we won't have to put on a religious mask. Then genuine, Christ-birthed righteousness will begin to flow out of our innermost beings and our worship will be unpretentious and sincere.

DIG YOUR WELL

"So," you may ask, "how do we start the journey of becoming authentic in our walk and relationship with God?" When you spend time with Him every day it's as if He gives you a shovel and you are digging a well. While you are worshiping, praying, reading the Word, listening, dancing, kneeling, or simply being still, you are building your relationship with Him. It's not difficult once you get underway. It's like any relationship. If I want to have a deep bond with my wife, I need to recognize that it won't happen automatically. We have to make it happen. If we want to go out on a date, we have to get a babysitter and drive somewhere. If we stay home, we talk with each other—with the television off. We write each other notes or text each other during the day. We pray together and serve each other. Over time, we are building a great marriage.

In the same way, as you are spending quality time with God, you are deepening your relationship, making it stronger—like digging a well. The ultimate goal is to keep digging until you strike water. Striking water represents that moment when you have a true connection or encounter with God. It may be hard to put into words, but it is a real and recognizable moment. Whether or not you get goose bumps or some other sensation, it will be a moment when you realize in your spirit that you actually *mean* what you are currently singing or saying. It can happen when you come across a Scripture that you must have read a hundred times before, and now, suddenly, you understand it in a whole new light.

The Holy Spirit, the Spirit of God, the person of God who dwells inside you, is the water. The very river of the living water of God is flowing through you (see John 7:39), and it is renewing you from the inside out. When you strike water, it washes over you, and it is refreshing. It is powerful. It is full of life. It is supernatural.

The water of the Spirit of God fills you up to the point of overflowing, but that does not mean that it is time to quit digging. In Pentecostal circles, people use the terms "tarry" and "press in." Don't stop. Keep seeking. Keep pursuing. Stay there, relating to God until you become so *full* of Him that it's impossible to continue being the old you. Let your thirst for the water of His presence drive you closer. In His presence, you become exactly the way He designed you to be.

POUR IT OUT

When you are in private, it's as if you have a well-digging shovel. But once you go out in public, you are carrying a pitcher instead. That means that when you go out, any place from the post office to the church, from the gas station to the streets, you are able to draw from your inner well and pour out pure, authentic refreshment on everyone around you.

Of course, if it has been some time since you've spent time digging your well, you may find that the water has become stagnant or stale, polluted or contaminated—teeming with the worries and cares of this life. Whatever you find in your well is what you will have available to pour out of your pitcher into the lives of others.

If it has been a long time since you spent an extended time alone with God, or if you've been relying on your times with God in the past or the time you spend in corporate worship, your well may be cracked and even empty. If so, you will find yourself at great risk of putting on the mask of pompous super-spirituality. You may feel almost obligated to play the part, to act "holier than thou." With nothing in your well to draw from, you may try to compensate, and as a result you are likely to come across as fake or even pharisaical. Never mind if other mask-wearing Christians are so used to church lingo that they do not recognize what is going on. (Together, we will all provide justification for those people who decide to stay away from church because of "those pharisaical Christians.")

Of course we never think of ourselves as Pharisees. We always see ourselves as the good guys in the story, and we view the Pharisees as the nasty villains. But if we stop and think about it, we have to realize that the Pharisees and other religious leaders in Jesus' day didn't think of themselves as the bad guys. They believed with all their hearts that they were doing exactly what God wanted. The fact is, if they could be deceived, so can we!

As humans, we are always tempted to put our energy into cleaning up or propping up the parts of our lives that other people see, instead of putting our energy into developing godly character. Naturally, we want people to see us fully mature in Christ, truly godly, and deeply spiritual. So we spit-shine our Sunday shoes in hope that people will see us as good Christians. We often justify this approach because we honestly do not want people to be discouraged by our "temporary" lack of spirituality. The actual truth is that we are deceiving both ourselves and them.

"Tomorrow," we promise ourselves, "I will definitely get up early enough to take a prayer time in the morning." But you know how it goes.... Tomorrow never comes. Even though we know we have slacked off, we reason that this is the exception to the rule. We just have not had time lately to get with God.

We carry so many responsibilities in ministry and in life, and we have so many demands on our time that we just have not been able to make space for the things of God. But we will...soon. Surely God understands all the demands on our life....

Little by little, we compromise, never planning on continuing in this fashion. Every day that goes by in which we break our promise to ourselves, we reinforce our habit of not spending time with God. Inevitably, the things that come up seem to be truly unforeseen circumstances. It never occurs to us to ask God for help, either. So we continue laboring under this "temporary" state, beautifying the outside of our spirituality even while the inside decays more and more, leaving less and less authentic substance to support our glorious eggshell exterior. Very sad, but often typical.

INSIDE OUT

Somehow, we do manage to find the time to polish our exterior, don't we? Yet we never seem to find enough time to work on the inside.

Jesus said something about this in the context of His commentary to the Pharisees. If we take it as solid advice, we should be able to gain great hope from it. He said,

> *How terrible it will be for you teachers of religious law and you Pharisees. Hypocrites! You are so careful to clean the outside of the cup and the dish, but inside you are filthy—full of greed and self-indulgence! Blind Pharisees! First wash the inside of the cup, and then the outside will become clean, too* (Matthew 23:25-26 NLT).

The secret Jesus has hidden in this passage can give us more of what we are looking for, more of the very thing we say we need so desperately—more ticks on the clock! Time. Time to spend with Him. Time to dig our wells. Time to be transformed by His living water. Time to be all He has called us to be.

It's easy to miss. Go back and read it again.

We need to put our emphasis in a new place. We have been putting the emphasis in the wrong place, spending so much time scrubbing and buffing the outside of the cup, the part everyone sees, that we never seem to find time to work on the inside. We use up all of our time in our efforts to perform according to impossible religious standards, while completely neglecting the inner issues of character, integrity, honestly, authenticity, and purity. Here Jesus discloses the secret: if we simply turn our energy from the outside of the cup to the inside of the cup—from the part everyone sees to the part nobody sees—He will take care of the part everyone sees, on our behalf.

This is like a miracle! If we concentrate on first things first ("*First*, wash the *inside* of the cup"), then everything else will take care of itself. It reminds me of a couple of other things that Jesus said:

> *Seek ye first the kingdom of God, and His righteousness; and all these things shall be added unto you* (Matthew 6:33 KJV).

> *For My yoke is easy, and My burden is light* (Matthew 11:30 KJV).

So, it's easier than we think. Instinctively, we may have realized it would be. Maybe that is why we are always looking for a shortcut. I don't know about you, but I always find myself hoping some preacher will show me a way to become godly that does not involve reading my Bible, praying, worshiping, and spending time in God's presence. Of course I have yet to find one who could do it.

Why do we make it so hard? Why do we resist doing the obvious? It's so simple. We have got to dig the well, dig the well, dig the well—the well of a true, authentic, genuine, pure, bona fide relationship with the Lord. Then, we will naturally cultivate a powerful private walk with God. And what is even more amazing is that this brings the peace of God with it. When you have spent time sitting at His feet like Mary, discovering the one thing that matters (see Luke

10:38-42)—then you can minister out of the overflow of the Spirit of God that truly dwells richly in you.

This is not only the way to become more godly; it is the way to become more authentically *you*. This is the way to become the person you have always wanted to be.

Have you ever wanted to be a person who is unashamed to share the Gospel, anyplace, anytime? How is this going to happen in you—through magic? I don't think so. You may pray, "Lord, make me bold and unafraid to share my faith," but you will have to do your part, which is to cultivate the transformation on the inside. You must develop your private walk with God, without taking shortcuts. Then, you will find yourself pouring out your heart in love to someone in need, remembering Scriptures you didn't even know you knew and wisdom you didn't even realize you had cultivated! It will have grown up inside you, because you planted it there.

Why do we think we are going to miss out on something if we spend so much time with God? We will never ever regret cultivating our relationship with Him. We will *never* look back and say, "Man, I wish I hadn't spent all that time digging the well of relationship with God. It really made me miss out on life!" In fact, when we are lying on our death beds we may do the exact opposite. I asked my godly grandmother, just before she died, what she would do differently if she could change her life. Without missing a beat, she said, "I would have read my Bible more!"

It's simple, but I am not saying it is easy. In fact, it is a huge challenge. It is easier for me to author this chapter than to spend time with the Author of Salvation. Every day I have to lecture myself, "Jeff, you don't feel like getting up out of bed, but you are going to get up out of this bed, and you are going to go downstairs to your office and spend time with Jesus."

If I keep spending the time on my first priority—Him—I can be sure that I will become everything I should be for my wife, my boys, my church family, and everyone who knows me. I will become the pure and true worshiper I was designed to be: righteous, holy and sanctified, refined, conformed and purified—everything I need to be before God, so that (see 1 Cor. 9:27) I will not be disqualified from spending eternity with my Lord and my God after working so hard to ensure the salvation of everyone else.

ETERNITY TO ETERNITY

(© Jeff Deyo)

Isaiah 43:13

You turn the night into a sunrise
You melt my heart with every touch.
You turn the tide when every hope seems lost.
You hold us all within Your hands.
From eternity to eternity
You preside over all
In Your majesty
You have purchased me
Loved me jealously;
You abide in our hearts
Ever more.

You turn the hearts of kings and kingdoms.
You're reaching out to every child.
You turn a light to every darkened soul;
You hold us all within Your hands.
You spoke a word and made the heavens.
You broke the power of sin and death.

No other god can now oppose You, Lord;
You hold us all within Your hands.

ENDNOTE

1. Paul Baloche, Jimmy and Carol Owens, *God Songs: How to Write and Select Songs for Worship* (Lindale, TX: Leadworship.com, 2004), 23.

Section Three

TIPS FOR THE JOURNEY

And Mary said: "My soul exalts the Lord, and my spirit has rejoiced in God my Savior. For He has had regard for the humble state of His bondslave; for behold, from this time on all generations will count me blessed. For the Mighty One has done great things for me; and holy is His name" (Luke 1:46-49 NASB).

We can agree with the prophetic Magnificat of Mary, *"The Mighty One has done great things for me."* But did you notice what else Mary stated here? *"For He has had regard for the humble state of His bondslave."* In the words of Mary we can find a significant tip for successful worshiping warriors. Humility.

The lost art of pure worship is more than just a great skill set. It is a constant issue of the heart. It includes wisdom and humility. The psalmist said,

Who may ascend into the hill of the Lord? And who may stand in His holy place? He who has clean hands and a pure heart, who has not lifted up his soul to falsehood and has not sworn deceitfully. He shall receive a blessing from the Lord and righteousness

from the God of his salvation. This is the generation of those who seek Him... (Psalm 24:3-6 NASB).

Chapter Eight

CREATING A CULTURE OF WORSHIP

RACHEL GOLL TUCKER

*L*ife is entirely too short to waste it without making an impact on our society. We were created to walk in righteousness, to exemplify and represent God in all of His wondrous ways, and to be salt and light in this world. Yet how can we influence a society that is so content with living and breathing in its own sickness?

We need to do something before it is too late. Our society is crying out through its rampant illness and its cycles of sin. It needs us to stop being passive and ashamed about following Christ and to start showing them what God is really like. We know that the only way we can have any degree of influence is through the power of God; He is our solution to everything. And I would like to suggest that you and I can penetrate our culture and cause true transformation through something as simple as worshiping Him.

My goal in this chapter is to break down a few simple ways that we as followers of Christ can live a lifestyle of worship. The rewards of this kind of worship far surpass the few moments of bliss or peace we may experience on Sunday mornings or Wednesday nights. This kind of worship entails a constant giving up of our sinful ways and a calling forth of the Spirit of God within us. This is more than a lifestyle—it is a *culture*. This has been a goal of my life from an early age and it will be the consuming goal of the rest of my life.

Together with each other and with God, we can start a worship culture, and we can expect the secular culture around us to take notice of that kind of Kingdom dynamic. For the most part, our neighbors and co-workers are walking in the dark. Let's give them a glimpse of the light of God's glory. No darkness is too deep for His light to penetrate. As C.S. Lewis wrote: "A man can no more diminish God's glory by refusing to worship Him than a lunatic can put out the sun by scribbling the word, 'darkness' on the walls of his cell."[1]

WORSHIPING WITH YOUR WORDS

In July of 2008 I moved to New York City to be a part of a month-long summer acting intensive for film and television at the New York Conservatory for Dramatic Arts. I had graduated a year early from high school and had already completed modeling school and one year of basic classes at a small community college, but I had never lived away from home.

My life changed very quickly as I went from living out in the country outside of Nashville, Tennessee, to living in a student housing apartment in Brooklyn Heights. The students in my program had come from Australia to Canada and everywhere in between. Our classes included Actor's Lab, Scene Study, Improvisation, Combat for Film, and Movement. It was quite the start to a new life, but I adjusted well, and I found myself with a roommate who loved and feared the Lord.

The month was passing quickly as I learned everything from how to stage fight on camera to breath control for acting, but we still had one final performance to do. In our Actor's Lab class we were each given a scene and a character to play. I was assigned a scene in which I would act with two other girls in my class. One girl was from Canada and the other was from the States. Both were questioning their sexuality. (But I didn't mind that too much because I was just grateful that my instructor had not assigned me the heated romance scene where I would have had to make out with the male lead. No thank you!)

As I learned my scene and started to develop my character, I began to run into a conflict within myself. My lines included a large number of curse words that I was uncomfortable with saying. My plan was to deliver the lines with the actual curse words only when we performed the scene for the final time. I had even told one of the actresses that I was not planning to practice with the actual curse words. To my surprise she replied, "Oh yeah; that's totally fine. You know, I was raised that way too." It saddened my heart to hear that she was raised that way, but she wasn't living it out.

The problem was, though, that the sick feeling in my stomach wouldn't go away as long as I kept going back and forth between compromising and sticking to my guns. The date to perform was getting closer and closer. Many times, I felt the temptation to go against my conscience and just say the words. *What's the harm?* I reasoned. *I don't really mean the words. They're just words. They aren't really going to hurt anyone.*

And yet I had read in my International Standard Version Bible, *"Let no filthy talk be heard from your mouths, but only what is good for building up people and meeting the need of the moment. This way you will administer grace to those who hear you"* (Eph. 4:29 ISV). And I had grown up hearing Romans 12:1, which reads, *"Therefore, I urge you, brothers and sisters, in view of God's mercy, to offer your bodies as a living sacrifice, holy and pleasing to God—this is your true and proper worship."*

These Scriptures dramatically came alive to me when my brother, Tyler, called me on the phone and simply said, "Rachel, don't do it. Don't start cursing." I was caught completely off guard, because not only did he address the place of contention within my heart, but he also had no idea about my current situation. I later found out that the Lord had given him a warning dream in which I returned home from New York and was cursing all the time and was not acting like my normal lively self.

Tyler's call was a nudge from the Holy Spirit that gave me enough courage to talk to my instructor and ask if I could change my lines that had cursing in them. When I did, my teacher agreed immediately and even made an announcement to the entire class saying, "If any of you are uncomfortable with any of the curse words in your script, you have the freedom to change them if you like." It was so simple! All I had to do was ask! I didn't have to curse in my script anymore and another girl chose to change hers, too!

Now, you may ask, what does something as simple as cursing or not cursing have to do with having a pure heart in worship? Everything! If you have invited Jesus into your heart, then your body is a temple for His dwelling place. That's what the apostle Paul said:

> *Or do you not know that your body is a temple of the Holy Spirit who is in you, whom you have from God, and that you are not your own? For you have been bought with a price: therefore glorify God in your body* (1 Corinthians 6:19-20 NASB).

We have the great joy to worship the King with what we allow ourselves to say and do. We worship Him (or not) with everything that we do in our bodies. We glorify Him as we strive to become more and more like Him in our speech and in our behavior. This is part of creating a sustained culture of worship where you attract the Holy Spirit's presence.

LOVE SONGS

The day after I returned home from New York, my sister, a neighbor of ours, and I were busy making one giant pancake in our kitchen when I got a phone call from the New York Conservatory for Dramatic Arts. They told me that I had been chosen for one of the few spots that they had left for the two-year Conservatory Program that was starting in a little over a week!

Thousands of aspiring actors and actresses from all around the world had auditioned for one of these spots at the school, so this was a huge opportunity for me.

After getting the blessing from my mother, who was sick in the hospital, and my more-than-excited father, I chose to cancel going back to the local community college in favor of going to study the art of acting in the Big Apple. All in all, the decision was made in a few hours, and I moved back to New York within a few days.

On the outside everything appeared to be the same, but little did I know how much different this experience would be. I moved back to the corner of Clark and Henry Street into the old 1920s celebrity hotel, which is now used for student housing. I shared a tiny room with another girl from Tennessee, who we'll call Sarah. Sarah was a sweet girl in her heart, but she couldn't have been more different from my previous roommate. Her boyfriend at the time was in jail in Memphis for who knows what. I had to learn to live with the F word being said every sentence that she spoke. While she wasn't attending school, she worked at a sex shop in Manhattan called Tic Tac Toe. This became my new "normal life."

Sarah had a friend named "Albert," who constantly came by our room to see her. He was 16 years old, and he had run away from his home in Liverpool to attend the acting school. He too was one of the few they had chosen from the month-long summer session that I had attended. His parents were divorced, with his father living in Australia and his mother in England. From the start he rubbed me the wrong way. I could not stand his presence in our apartment with his constant crass jokes, foul mouth, and occasional high state from the use of drugs. He was bad news to me, but he wouldn't stop coming to see Sarah.

One night when Albert came walking into our room I was preoccupied playing guitar and singing. He said, "Rachel, play me a song." I thought of all of the songs I knew, and I remembered that the Lord had recently been speaking to me to start playing a simple song that I had written called "Stained." So without giving it too much thought I began to sing...

I can't get the memory of you
To go away
I can't get the fragrance of you
Out of my clothes
You have stained me
You have stained this heart
You have stained me
And you'll always remain
I can find a catastrophe
That could distract your love for me
I can't find a melody
That's not reminiscent of you
You have stained me
You have stained this heart
You have stained me
And you'll always remain.

After I finished singing the song, Albert asked me, "Did you write that for a boyfriend?"

My heart sank as I fumbled through my words, saying, "No, it's not written for anyone really." I had just lied straight to his face! The truth was that I had written that song as a love song from my heart to the Lord. I didn't know what to do with his question, so I ended up denying that the song was even written for anyone.

When the night settled and I was lying in my cold twin-size bed across from my roommate, I felt the Lord whisper to me. He said, "Next time Albert asks you to play 'Stained,' tell him the truth. Tell him you wrote it for Me."

Why is it sometimes so much easier to lie than to tell the truth? Matthew 5:37 says, *"All you need to say is simply 'Yes' or 'No'; anything beyond this comes from the evil one."* We as Christians need to live by the high standard of the Word of Truth! When we do this, our worship does not just go upward to God, but His influence becomes evident to others when they see us living a lifestyle that's beyond being just a "good person." They will know that we are lovers and followers of Jesus.

Later, the next time Albert requested that song, I did end up telling him the truth about it. I also took the opportunity, every time he or any of my other friends asked for that song, to sing it to my Creator and the lover of my soul. I worshiped Him right in front of them. No longer could I sing my love songs to the Lord only in secret; I knew that He wanted the love songs of my heart to reflect Him and be shown to the world.

I took another Scripture to heart. Jesus said,

> *You are the salt of the earth. But if the salt loses its saltiness, how can it be made salty again? It is no longer good for anything, except to be thrown out and trampled underfoot.*
>
> *You are the light of the world. A town built on a hill cannot be hidden. Neither do people light a lamp and put it under a bowl. Instead they put it on its stand, and it gives light to everyone in the house. In the same way, let your light shine before others, that they may see your good deeds and glorify your Father in heaven* (Matthew 5:13-16).

A year or so later, Albert contacted me and told me that he had started following the Lord. I have not kept up with him since my New York days, but I trust that the seeds that the Lord allowed me to sow were in His timing and for a good purpose, and I know that we are *all* worth it. You never know...sometimes in the most unlikely of circumstances and with the strangest of people, that could be exactly when the Lord chooses to influence somebody through you. This is the power that a sustained culture of worship creates—change in other people's lives.

WORSHIPING WITH YOUR TALENTS

If someone is a songwriter, Nashville, Tennessee, is the place to be. When my husband, McKendree Augustas Tucker IV, was 23 years old, he made the move from St. Simon's Island, Georgia, to the Tennessee music capital of the country. He went through many struggles like the ones I experienced in New York, but that didn't stop his desire to pursue his dream of playing and writing music to glorify God.

One of the most discouraging questions he (or anybody else who's trying to make a way in the world of entertainment) got asked was, "Do you know the percentage of people who actually make it big?" The answer, of course, is a very low percentage. But sometimes it isn't about "making it big" or "becoming popular." Sometimes it is simply and completely about living out the desires and dreams that the Lord has placed within you. In fact, Jesus told a parable about this:

> *Again, it will be like a man going on a journey, who called his servants and entrusted his wealth to them. To one he gave five bags of gold, to another two bags, and to another one bag, each according to his ability. Then he went on his journey. The man who had received five bags of gold went at once and put his money to work and gained five bags more. So also, the one with two bags of gold gained two more. But the man who had received one bag went off, dug a hole in the ground and hid his master's money.*
>
> *After a long time the master of those servants returned and settled accounts with them. The man who had received five bags of gold brought the other five. "Master," he said, "you entrusted me with five bags of gold. See, I have gained five more." His master replied,*

"Well done, good and faithful servant! You have been faithful with a few things; I will put you in charge of many things. Come and share in your master's happiness!"

The man with two bags of gold also came. "Master," he said, "you entrusted me with two bags of gold; see, I have gained two more."

His master replied, "Well done, good and faithful servant! You have been faithful with a few things; I will put you in charge of many things. Come and share your master's happiness!"

Then the man who had received one bag of gold came. "Master," he said, "I knew that you are a hard man, harvesting where you have not sown and gathering where you have not scattered seed. So I was afraid and went out and hid your gold in the ground. See, here is what belongs to you."

His master replied, "You wicked, lazy servant! So you knew that I harvest where I have not sown and gather where I have not scattered seed? Well then, you should have put my money on deposit with the bankers, so that when I returned I would have received it back with interest.

"So take the bag of gold from him and give it to the one who has ten bags. For whoever has will be given more, and they will have an abundance. Whoever does not have, even what they have will be taken from them. And throw that worthless servant outside, into the darkness, where there will be weeping and gnashing of teeth" (Matthew 25:14-30).

I believe God has given each and every person a unique set of skills and talents. Not all of us are supposed to be songwriters or worship leaders, but all of us can worship God by offering our talents to Him, whatever they may be.

Some people might be gifted in cooking, knowledge, organization, fine arts, or even showing kindness. But what happens when that gifted dancer never uses her gift? Or that brilliant accountant is held back by fear? The expression of God within them never gets let out.

God is not glorified when we do nothing with the talents that He has given us. We might be considered the "wicked and lazy servant." Not only that, but we may see the talent that we squandered get stripped from us and given to someone else who wants to steward it.

On the flip side, when we are diligent with the gifts He has given us, He says, "Well done, good and faithful servant! You have been faithful with a few things; I will put you in charge of many things. Come and share your master's happiness!"

I don't know about you, but I want to be one who shares in my Father's happiness! You can learn to worship the Lord through your gifts and talents that He has entrusted to you—*no matter* what your talent is. You may wonder, "How can I worship God with this mere hobby or meager talent?" You can give Him your all!

As Jesus said, *"Love the Lord your God with all your heart and with all your soul and with all your mind.' This is the first and greatest commandment"* (Matt. 22:37-38). Usually we get the heart part, while we forget about the soul and mind part. But those elements are a vital part of giving your all to the Lord. If we want to create a lifestyle of worship, we need to submit *all* that we are.

A lifestyle is a whole way of living, and it reflects the values and attitudes that a person subscribes to. As Christians, our lifestyles should reflect our love for the Lord. What if every Christian walked out every day reflecting the Lord through worship, with all that "worship" means? What if worship became our "new normal" lifestyle? Then we could truly create a culture of worship, and it would make a difference in the world around us.

LIVE A LIFE WORTHY OF THE CALLING

In June of 2009, I met the man that I would one day call my husband. He had come a long way from when he had first moved to Nashville. He had become the keyboard player for the band Sonicflood, and he was also doing his own music and production on the side.

Quickly, we discovered that the Lord had placed the same thread in both of our hearts, which was making an impact on the entertainment industry through song. Both of us had felt the Father's heart for Hollywood, and we had wept tears over its salvation. We thought, *What if together we could write music that is filled with the Holy Spirit that would infiltrate the darkest of places?* We combined our lives with a simple goal in mind: whether we are leading a worship song on a Sunday morning or playing a secular love song at a coffee shop, we want the Lord to be glorified.

That was the dream the Lord had placed inside our hearts, and we are now pursuing it. After living in Nashville for a season, we now reside in Chambersburg, Pennsylvania, where McKendree is serving as a contemporary worship pastor. We have the honor of leading people into the presence of the Lord at church and also playing our secular love songs at various other venues.

We are still in our twenties, but this journey has already been quite an extraordinary one. I have learned that you never know where He is going to lead you next, so you have to get ready by honing the skills the Lord has entrusted you with, preparing your heart to carry truth in your words, and being courageous—for we have the biggest and greatest Dad in the whole wide world backing us up! We need to believe that He didn't place those dreams in our hearts for nothing.

Now that you and I have Christ, we have nothing left to lose. He is all we need. Let's just run into His arms and let Him guide us as we chase after the dreams He has placed in our hearts. Our circumstances may challenge our resolve, but we need to listen to Paul, who wrote to the Christians in Ephesus when he was in prison: *"As a prisoner for the Lord, then, I urge you to live a life worthy of the calling you have received"* (Eph. 4:1).

As we live a lifestyle of worship, we will find ourselves in the most unearthly and heavenly relationship with the Creator. He beckons for us to come to His throne in worship and adoration through every expression given by Him in our hearts, souls, and minds. As we respond to His call each and every day and make it our lifestyle, we create a culture of worship.

GIVE UP EVERYTHING

(© Rachel Tucker, www.augustyork.com)

We put our hope in the Living God
Who is the Savior of all men.
We put our trust in His promises
Who holds our dreams in His hands.
And I will trust You, Lord
I will trust You, Lord
I will give up everything to be like my King.
I will shine bright like He does.
I will give up everything to be like my King.
I will go forth and make disciples.

ENDNOTE

1. From *The Problem of Pain*, by C.S. Lewis, originally published in 1940, copyright restored in 1996.

Chapter Nine

THE PROPHETIC SONG
OF THE LORD

JAMES W. GOLL

One time when I was ministering in Germany, the Holy Spirit gave me a dream about the power of the Pied Piper. So I had to do research to find out the background of this interesting character and his meaning for us today.

The German town of Hamlin was infested with rats. In the story of the Pied Piper, set in 1284, a stranger in pied (multi-colored) clothing offered to get rid of them for a stated sum. The city officials agreed. The stranger proceeded to walk through the streets playing a pipe (a flute), and the rats poured out of every hiding place to follow him. He led them into the river, where they drowned. But the officials reneged on their promise to pay, enraging the piper with their double-dealing. The piper picked up his instrument and again walked through the streets. This time, it was the children of the town who followed him. He led them to a mountain that opened to receive them and then closed after them. The children were never seen again. An entire generation had been lost.

We can see this story in a positive light by putting on a redemptive, prophetic lens, recognizing that something similar has happened in this past generation. Music has been used both for good and for evil, and an entire generation of young people has followed blindly after it. Music has enticing spiritual power, and only musicians whose motives are pure will be able to lead others deeper into God. It is time for God's Holy-Spirit-anointed pipers to come along and to play the songs of Heaven on earth and capture the hearts of a generation. True spiritual warfare will result, and we will drive the rats out of our cities and regions. Yes, music carries a powerful influence.

We read in First Chronicles 15:22 and 27 about a priest named Chenaniah (or "Kenaniah") who was chosen to be the leader of the levitical musicians because of his skill in music. Along with the honor came a responsibility to lead the other priests and the people of Israel closer to God. Pure worship was the goal then, and it is our goal today. One of the sometimes "unsung" aspects of pure worship is what we call the "song of the Lord." Is this a part of the missing arsenal needed today to win a generation back to Jesus?

WHAT IS THE SONG OF THE LORD?

In a general sense, all worship that is sung to music is the song of the Lord. Different terms are often used to describe the same or similar expressions of this creative musical art form: "a new song," a "prophetic song," as well as a song of (or to) the Lord. Many times, such songs spring up spontaneously at first, under the inspiration of the Holy Spirit, and they remain songs of the Lord even after being written down and sung over and over. If you add the word *prophetic* to the phrase, it indicates that the song of the Lord has taken on a prophetic voice, speaking of the future and what God wants to do in the midst of the people, or a relevant message from His heart in the now. It pierces through the crust of religion and brings God into the present tense.

The words of these precious songs of the Lord can represent the Lord singing to His people as well as His people singing songs of praise to Him. The Book of

Psalms contains many songs of the Lord, as do other books of the Bible. Here's a good example from the Book of Zephaniah:

Sing, Daughter Zion; shout aloud, Israel! Be glad and rejoice with all your heart, Daughter Jerusalem! The Lord has taken away your punishment, He has turned back your enemy. The Lord, the King of Israel, is with you; never again will you fear any harm. On that day they will say to Jerusalem, "Do not fear, Zion; do not let your hands hang limp. The Lord your God is with you, the Mighty Warrior who saves. He will take great delight in you; in His love He will no longer rebuke you, but will rejoice over you with singing" (Zephaniah 3:14-17).

Other earlier scriptural songs that have been recorded for us include the song of Moses (the first recorded song of the Lord) in Exodus 15:1-19, the song of Miriam in Exodus 15:20, the lengthy second song of Moses in Deuteronomy 31:19-22, 30; 32:1-43, and the song of Israel at the well in Numbers 21:16-18 ("Spring up, oh well!"). We have another song of victory in the duet singing of Deborah and Barak concerning Jael and Sisera (see the entire fifth chapter of Judges).

My late wife, Michal Ann, and I used to sing spontaneous songs together in a similar duet fashion, weaving together lyrics prophetically given at the moment, blending unique harmonies, each not knowing where the other one was going, and yet always creating a beautiful stream of pure worship unto the King of Hearts. This was one of our greatest joys as partners in Christ, singing the "now song" to and from the Lord.

The Bible is filled with songs and more songs. The Book of Job declares that the morning stars were singing (see Job 38:4-7) and the Book of Jonah mentions a song of thanksgiving (see Jon. 2:9).

Consider Isaiah's many songs of the Lord:

- the song of the Beloved and His vineyard (see Isa. 5:1)

- the song of praise (see Isa. 12:1-6)

- the song of the strong city (see Isa. 26:1-4)

- the joyful songs of the redeemed (see Isa. 35:1-10)

- the "new song" of the Lord (see Isa. 42:10)

- the song of joy in creation (see Isa. 44:23)

- the song of salvation (see Isa. 52:7-12)

- the song of the suffering savior (see Isa. 53:1-12)

Hezekiah, Jeremiah, and Ezekiel wrote about or recorded the actual words for several songs with themes ranging from salvation, rescue, protection, and thanksgiving to mournful rejection. (See Isaiah 38:20, Psalms 120–134, Jeremiah 31:12-13, and Ezekiel 33:32.)

Then of course we have all of the songs of David and his son, Solomon—a staggering number. David wrote many of the psalms, and he appointed singers to lead the people in continual worship (see 1 Chron. 16:7). As many as 1,005 songs have been attributed to King Solomon, besides the entire book of the Bible that we know as the "Song of Songs" or "Song of Solomon." (See First Kings 4:29-34.) Some of David's songs were incorporated into the Bible more than once. Look, for example, at Second Samuel 22, with its distinct echoes of the song of deliverance that is more familiar to us as Psalm 18:

The Lord is my rock, my fortress and my deliverer; my God is my rock, in whom I take refuge, my shield and the horn of my salvation. He is my stronghold, my refuge and my savior.... He parted the heavens and came down; dark clouds were under His feet. He mounted the cherubim and flew; He soared on the wings of the wind. He made darkness His canopy around Him—the dark rain clouds of the sky.... You have delivered me from the attacks of the peoples; You have preserved me as the head of nations. People I did not know now serve me, foreigners cower before me; as soon as they hear of me, they obey me. They all lose heart; they come trembling from their strongholds. The Lord lives! Praise be to my Rock! Exalted be my God, the Rock, my Savior! (2 Samuel 22:2-3, 10-12, 44-47)

In the New Testament we have the song of the Messiah in the Church, taken from the words of Psalm 22:22, 25: *"I will proclaim Your name to my brethren; in the midst of the congregation I will sing Your praise"* (Heb. 2:12 NASB).

We can read about singing men and women throughout the Bible. See, for example, Exodus 15:20 (Miriam and her rejoicing women), First Chronicles 25:5-6, Ecclesiastes 2:8, and Ezra 2:64-65 (which reads, *"The whole company* [the exiles who returned to Jerusalem] *numbered 42,360, besides their 7,337 male and female slaves; and they also had 200 **male and female singers"***). We see male and female singers also in Nehemiah 7:67, Second Samuel 19:35, Second Chronicles 35:25. Moving on into the New Testament time frame, the people of God were encouraged to keep on singing: *"Sing and make music from your heart to the Lord"* (Eph. 5:19), and *"Let the message of Christ dwell among you richly as you teach and admonish one another with all wisdom through psalms, hymns, and songs from the Spirit, singing to God with gratitude in your hearts"* (Col. 3:16).

We must not forget to mention the songs of the redeemed in the Book of Revelation (see the "new song" in Revelation 5:8-9 and 14:2-3), as well as the song of Moses and the Lamb (see Rev. 15:3-4). God seems to have created people to sing songs to and about Him! We can only conclude that the Word of God is full of the "song of the Lord."

MINDFUL OF THE TABERNACLE

Throughout this book, we have written about the present-day restoration of the tabernacle of David. While we have made it clear that we do not intend to restore the physical tabernacle, reviewing the God-ordained structure of the tabernacle of Moses can teach us a lot about how to approach God in worship.

Like the priests in the Old Testament, our worship can follow the same progressive pattern of walking through the tabernacle and into the presence of God.

As you know, God's purpose is always the same—to bring people to Himself—and the structure of the tabernacle of Moses (restored by David) reflects both His purpose and His nature so that people can understand how to respond to Him.

Through the tabernacle of Moses, we see shadows and types of New Testament realities. That original tabernacle had three sections: the outer court, the holy place, and the most holy place. (See many of the very specific instructions of God to Moses in chapters 25–27 of Exodus.) Only the high priest was allowed into the most holy place, and he had to take with him the blood of the sacrifice. Today, because of Jesus' perfect sacrifice, all believers now have the right of direct access into the equivalent of the most holy place—the place where God dwells:

> *Therefore, brothers and sisters, since we have confidence to enter the Most Holy Place by the blood of Jesus, by a new and living way opened for us through the curtain, that is, His body, and since we have a great priest over the house of God, let us draw near to God with a sincere heart and with the full assurance that faith brings, having our hearts sprinkled to cleanse us from a guilty conscience and having our bodies washed with pure water* (Hebrews 10:19-22).

In the outer court, the brazen altar represents Christ's sacrifice for sin, and the brazen laver represents the cleansing power of God's Word. In the holy place, the table of shewbread represents Jesus Christ, the Bread of Life, and the lampstand represents the Church, which casts its light upon Him. The altar of incense stands for the ministry of praise and worship, which is the main theme of this book. And the most holy place, which contains the ark of the covenant and the presence of God Himself, represents Christ and His mercy seat. (The original ark contained Moses' tablets of stone, Aaron's rod that budded, and a pot of manna.) The gold covering the ark represents purity.

Pure worship. Entering the inner court (meaning access to the most holy place, the presence of God) could be attained only through the blood of the sacrifice, accompanied by the incense of praise and worship:

> *Shout joyfully to the Lord, all the earth. Serve the Lord with gladness; come before Him with joyful singing.... Enter His gates with thanksgiving and His courts with praise. Give thanks to Him, bless His name* (Psalm 100:1-2, 4 NASB).

In the same way, the outpoured Holy Spirit in our lives should result in ongoing, ever-increasing worship coming from hearts that have been so profoundly touched by God. And yet we are "leaky vessels." We need to replenish what we lose and even reverse the leakage through more worship and, as a result, more of His presence, even as we grow in demonstrating aspects of the pure character of God in our lives.

As we worship with abandon, we become more like our heavenly counterparts, and our worship becomes even more pure. As we re-center ourselves on the One who deserves all of our praise, we grow in His character traits. Wisdom and insight accrue to our heavenly bank accounts. His presence becomes our passion and eventually even our companion.

God displays His character in us as the fruit of the Spirit and the power (gifts) of the Spirit. As He has His way in our lives, we cannot help but express our joy and gratitude with even more worship, singing "psalms and hymns and spiritual songs" (see Eph. 5:19). We sing songs that are both old and new, some of which are well-established in Christian circles and others of which have been freshly minted as prophetic songs of the Lord.

What is the goal of the prophetic song of the Lord? The goal is simply that we would repent and be restored to God. Prophetic declarations, whether spoken or sung, are invitations to repent of sin and lukewarm living, to change and improve our direction, and to grow in life-sustaining belief and obedience.

The power of these declarations is amazing. It is like going into a house where darkness prevails, but as soon as you turn on the light switch, darkness flees. When you sing the song of the Lord, darkness lifts and the glory of the Lord arises upon you, your house, and your sphere of influence. Why not turn on the lights in your house right now?

HOW TO RECEIVE AND SING THE SONG OF THE LORD

Today, our access to God's presence is not limited by artifacts and ceremonies. Under the New Covenant, not only can we come directly into God's presence, we can decide when to do it. We can "practice His presence," and one of the best ways to do it is through worshiping in song. We can practice singing songs to and from the Lord, both in private and in corporate times of worship. After first quieting our souls before Him, we can turn words of praise into a song, or take a Scripture and turn it into a song. The psalms are easiest to use, of course, because the lyrics are already written out for us; all we need to supply is a new tune. We can also sing out our heartfelt intercession for others, or we can put to music a current testimony of the Lord's goodness. We can declare our devotion, express our yearning for Heaven, and much more.

Any of these expressions can be considered the prophetic song of the Lord, and they can enrich our worship greatly. We can "tune in" to the frequencies of Heaven's songs, listening with our hearts and asking, "What song is being sung in Heaven right now? What song does Heaven want to hear from earth right now?"

Our songs do not need to be of recording-studio quality. You do not need to possess an opera singer's voice. Sometimes you may only hum, or murmur a phrase, or even whistle. If you can play a musical instrument, you can "sing" to the Lord by playing it to Him, whether you use words or not. You can repeat a line over and over without losing the value of the words. ("Holy, holy, holy" is what they repeat in Heaven!) You can sing in any language, including the language of the Spirit, singing your prayers and high praises in tongues.

By beginning devotionally and expectantly, asking God to inspire your words and thoughts and melodies, you can join in with the heavenly choir that proclaims God's attributes unto eternity:

> *I will sing of the Lord's great love forever; with my mouth I will make Your faithfulness known through all generations. I will declare that Your love stands firm forever, that You have established Your faithfulness in heaven itself.... The heavens praise Your wonders, Lord, Your faithfulness too, in the assembly of the holy ones. For who in the skies above can compare with the Lord? Who is like the Lord among the heavenly beings? In the council of the holy ones God is greatly feared; He is more awesome than all who surround Him. Who is like You, Lord God Almighty? You, Lord, are mighty, and Your faithfulness surrounds You.... Blessed are those who have learned to acclaim You, who walk in the light of Your presence, Lord. They rejoice in Your name all day long; they celebrate Your righteousness. For You are their glory and strength...* (Psalm 89:1-2, 5-8, 15-17).

You can practice new melodies, as contented and unselfconscious as a mother who is rocking her infant and singing little love songs. Sing love melodies to the Lord. See how creative His Spirit will help you to be! Just do it from your heart.

Once, many years ago with Michal Ann, I was in a time of fasting and prayer and I felt that the Lord gave me the following lyrics, which were inspired from Isaiah 30:15 and Isaiah 40:28-31. An angel was released that night. He touched my side, and I was catapulted into a visionary state. He gave me an unusual melody that I remember to this day, although I cannot reproduce that within the pages of this book. This song has stayed with me over the years. Though it was a song for the moment, it became etched within my memory as a song for any moment:

> *In quietness and confidence shall be your strength.*
> *In quietness and confidence shall be your strength.*

You shall mount up with wings as the eagles.
You shall run and not faith.
You will walk and not be weary.
Wait. I say, wait.
In quietness and confidence shall be your strength.
In quietness and confidence shall be your strength.

You too can read and study the written Word with an eye to singing it back to Him. After all, many of the songs we find in Scripture started in just this way. As you get used to the process of receiving and singing songs of the Lord, you can step out in greater faith and confidence, asking the Lord for a tender heart and a greater sensitivity to the voice of His Spirit.

BECOME WHAT YOU SING

In addition, you can also become what you are singing about; you can become part of the message of the song. If you are singing about holiness, you will want to be holy yourself. If you're going to sing about comfort, let it cause you to become a comforter who gives comfort to others. If your song is about encouragement, go ahead and give some real encouragement to somebody else. Perhaps the song is an intercessory prayer put to music. You are identifying with the needs of your city, church, or nation, and you simply turn that heartfelt yearning for change into a melody unto the Lord. You can find a limitless number of ways to worship Him as you underline the purity of your worship by adding loving actions to your inspired songs of the Lord.

The prophetic song of the Lord is a responsive song. You turn your ear to His voice and He tells you something. When I go into a city for my next assignment, I ask the Holy Spirit to open my heart and my ear so I can hear what song the Messiah is redemptively singing over that city, congregation, people group, or nation. Then I can become His echo or megaphone, declaring His kind intentions in the earth realm. These kinds of prophetic songs of the Lord can often be used to help elevate the entire atmosphere into another realm, the "God zone," a sphere where His love is known and where all things are possible.

When we respond in pure worship-filled song, our songs rise like incense to Him, and He loves to hear them! How wonderful it is that we not only get to sing to Him, we also get to be His ambassadors and sing on His behalf wherever we may find ourselves.

Oh, how I love to sing the songs of Zion! Since my youth, this has been my primary passion. As stated earlier, before I was ever a prophet, a pastor, a teacher, or an author, I was a singer. And a priestly singer I will be until the day I pass through to the other side. I know that this is one ministry that will continue forever. I never plan to stop singing. For eternity, I will sing the song of and to the Lord.

Do you want a ministry that will be relevant in the here and now, as well as in the hereafter? Then let the prophetic song of the Lord become an integral part of your own life of pure worship.

NEARER MY GOD TO THEE

(by Sarah Fuller Flower Adams, public domain)

Nearer, my God, to Thee, nearer to Thee!
E'en though it be a cross that raiseth me,
Still all my song shall be, nearer, my God, to Thee.
Nearer, my God, to Thee,
Nearer to Thee!
Though like the wanderer, the sun gone down,
Darkness be over me, my rest a stone.
Yet in my dreams I'd be nearer, my God to Thee.

There let the way appear, steps unto heav'n;
All that Thou sendest me, in mercy given;
Angels to beckon me nearer, my God, to Thee.
Then, with my waking thoughts bright with Thy praise,
Out of my stony griefs Bethel I'll raise;
So by my woes to be nearer, my God, to Thee.
Or, if on joyful wing cleaving the sky,
Sun, moon, and stars forgot, upward I'll fly,
Still all my song shall be, nearer, my God, to Thee.
There in my Father's home, safe and at rest,
There in my Savior's love, perfectly blest;
Age after age to be, nearer my God to Thee.

Chapter Ten

WORSHIP ROAD TRIP

CHRIS DUPRÉ

Road trip! OK, let's take a journey, a road trip so to speak, of how worship has developed over the past 40 years. I believe that it is important for the people of every generation to see and know how God has been moving in their own generation, and tracking the development of worship is certainly a way to see God's heart and hand moving among His own.

I was saved in 1973, the tail end of what was known as the Jesus Movement. Coming out of a Catholic background, I had very little knowledge of church music. During my years growing up in our small town in Marion, New York, we used to sing a very limited number of hymns. Most songs were short antiphonal phrases in response to either the choir or the priest. When I arrived as a newly saved young man at a small Christian church in Brockport, New York, I was immediately introduced to two new forms of church music: classic hymns and worship choruses.

What a trip it was the first time I ever entered the church. It was a Friday night and the church was filled with college-age kids, singing, clapping, and acting very excited to be there. I looked around and found myself in another world. A band was on stage leading worship, but it was not your typical band. They sang with a freedom and an abandonment that I had never seen before.

My first thought was, *Wow, they sure seem to be having a lot of fun.* But as worship progressed, something else began to happen. The Spirit of God was filling the room with His presence, something I had never experienced before. Hearts were softening, and you could tangibly see the focus of people's hearts shift from themselves to Him. By the time worship was over, there were tears running down a number of cheeks.

As I said, this was all new to me. I loved music as much as the next person did, but neither Led Zeppelin nor the Allman Brothers had ever had this effect on me. This was something else. It was more than music. It was an exchange of affection—God pursuing us so that we would pursue Him.

I ended up moving there a few months later. And because I could play the guitar and sing, I was invited to join that same group I had heard the first time I had visited. I loved it. We would play every Friday night, and this little building that could barely hold 200 people would be bulging with at least 250 to 300 worshipers every week.

A DECADE OF SIMPLE PRAISE

Back then there was little in terms of new worship music to learn and incorporate. Maranatha Music on the West Coast was the primary stream of contemporary worship music. Chuck Gerrard and Love Song were the cutting edge sound of what we would now call Contemporary Christian Music. Though they both offered some very wonderful music, it was a drop in the bucket as compared to what is available today.

With my very limited understanding of contemporary church music, I began to learn what was out there, and to be honest, what was out there was very limited. Most songs consisted of three chords, mostly in the key of D or G. The rhythms were so similar that you could do a half-dozen songs in a row and never change the key or the rhythm. But for some reason that did not matter. Almost every time we led, there was an explosion of worship. People knew the songs so well yet the power of the songs came not from the music, but from their human hearts.

Because I love ballads and sweet songs, I began to look for some more personal and tender songs to do during worship. People responded very positively to the songs I led and yet some church leaders encouraged me to do more upbeat songs, because they felt the "slower ones" might drag down the worship. Since 90 percent of our songs were upbeat, that wasn't hard to do.

However, this turned out to be the first time I disagreed with the people who were leading the college ministry. They wanted to keep an upbeat sound throughout almost the entire time of worship and yet I was seeing something else happen when we ventured into times of more intimate worship.

Though I wanted to do it my way, I learned a very valuable lesson. I was there to serve. If the leaders wanted upbeat songs, that is what I would do. It is an important step for anybody to take—to learn to serve the vision of someone else. When whatever we are doing is not all about us, we can grow in both humility and servanthood. Conversely, something unwanted enters the picture like a bad seed when our own preferences and agenda become our focus and desire.

I have heard worship leaders say, "Well, God gave me this music, so I need to get it out there. That's why He put me here as a worship leader." That may be one small reason why a worship leader is there, but the most important reason he or she is there is to serve everyone who walks into that church. You become their servant by creating an "on-ramp" for them to soar up into the arms of God.

At any rate, during the early seventies the worship music was not the focus of the day. There were new songs out there, but they were few and far between. You had to do a lot of searching to find a few really decent worship songs. I had been writing my own songs for a long time, so I continued to write, making worship songs my primary emphasis.

Looking back, I would say that the seventies were a decade of simple praise. Most of the music went in the direction of songs of thanksgiving and gratefulness for all God had done. When people come to understand what God had saved them from and what He had redeemed them for, they could do nothing but give Him the thanks and praise He deserved.

GROWTH AND EXPANSION OF WORSHIP SOUNDS

As the eighties arrived, I began to see that something more organized was coming to the Christian music industry. Though recorded worship music had existed before the eighties, it had been more in the background. The eighties brought it to the forefront. The tool that I believe was used more than any other during this time was Integrity Music. A more high-energy style of music, this mostly keyboard-driven sound found a home in churches all across the world.

Integrity Music was instrumental (no pun intended) in organizing, recording, and releasing to the church more worship music than ever before. It was amazing. You could even sign up and get it delivered to your door. Every six to eight weeks, a new tape (yes, I said tape) would arrive at my house and I would go find a secluded spot and listen to it. I loved the music, but I found myself much more interested in what I could use as worship music for my church.

That is why it was an eye-opener for me when the Lord began to challenge me about my motivation for getting the latest tape. I was initially confused by this but I began to see His wisdom for my life. He was less interested in how I would use the music and more interested in how the music would affect my heart. He's always after the heart, and we are much too often all about the ministry.

He showed me that if I wanted to use the music for leading others into His presence, it needed to be real to me first. It had to come alive in my heart before it would come alive in the hearts of others. All too often you can see a worship leader leading a song, yet you can tell by looking that to them it is just a song, not something that burns within them.

This may be very subtle sometimes, but it is a very important truth: we need to lead songs that we already "own" within our hearts. I always encourage people in the worship world that *we need to be lovers of God who happen to play music as opposed to musicians who happen to be Christians*. Otherwise, they will find themselves in a very slow slide toward having it be all about the music, instead of being all about Him.

A wonderful shift along those lines began to bear fruit in the mid- to late 1980s. The Vineyard movement had been underway for a few years and its leader, John Wimber (a former bass player with the Righteous Brothers), helped to usher in a less complicated style of worship, a style that was more guitar-driven and much more intimate as it focused less on singing *about* God and more on singing *to* Him. Even the language of the songs was more intimate, as tender lyrics spoke about a deep affection between the Father and His children.

For worship leaders who led on guitar, the Vineyard songs were a literal godsend. As Integrity songs became more complicated, the new Vineyard songs were much more easily translatable to most local churches. I had the pleasure of getting to meet with and talk to John Wimber and I quickly learned that one of his greatest pleasures was knowing the impact that the Vineyard worship music was having upon the local churches.

My love of the Vineyard music was not only due to the ease with which it could be introduced in the church, but because of the beauty of the songs. These simple songs gave us language in which to release our hearts to our heavenly Father. Suddenly we were not just singing songs of thanksgiving, but we were intimately communicating with our Father and friend.

As the Vineyard music grew in popularity, people across the globe began to follow in the footsteps of the Vineyard writers, penning their own songs of love and intimacy. This created a wave of creativity around the globe that unleashed more home-grown worship music than ever before.

Probably the part of the world that was the most influenced by all this was England. Soon, beautiful new music began pouring out of England. This music possessed the intimacy of the Vineyard music, and yet it carried a unique sound of its own. The first to come out was a series of tapes under the name Cutting Edge. This was the first offering brought forth by Martin Smith and the band that would soon be known as Delirious.

What made this music so inviting was the combination of intimate words mixed with a cutting-edge sound. Worship music could actually be sweet and fun at the same time! More writers followed as Matt Redman, Tim Hughes, and others created a new kind of British invasion. It was a welcomed invasion, for sure.

By the time the year 2000 came around, we no longer had only one or two main worship music movements. New music was coming from everywhere. And it was not just new lyrics, but also new styles and expressions. All of them were now represented in Christian music. Praise, adoration, and intimacy were now all part of the worship diet.

For too long, the church had been riding the coattails of the world's music. Now, Christians from all over were bringing forth beautiful and creative music that rivaled anything the world had to offer. In the midst of this, God continued to make sure that it was never to be about the music only. It's not the sound, the label, or the place that's important. It's always about Him.

FLOWING FROM HIM, TO HIM

In His response to the Samaritan woman's statement that her forefathers worshiped on a mountain, Jesus told her (see John 4) that worship was not supposed to be relegated to a specific mountain or to a place, even one that has been viewed as holy to so many, such as the city of Jerusalem.

Because the Father is seeking out people who would worship Him, worship is meant to be a personal, reciprocal expression of our faith and love toward Him. On God's part, His personal seeking out is akin to when He sought out Adam in the Garden. God's initial intent—and His desire to this day—was to have a personal relationship with men and women.

That is not the way we have set things up, although advertising, for instance, "Worship 10:30 A.M." is not wrong within itself. But when our systemization begins to replace that vital, reciprocal relationship with God, it can become dangerous.

Jesus went on to say to the Samaritan woman, *"God is spirit, and His worshipers must worship in the Spirit and in truth"* (John 4:24). He was speaking about how true worship must contain aspects of both spirit and truth, which does not mean expressing two opposing points of view, but rather is meant to show the power of two interwoven features, a symmetry, so to speak, that every person needs in living life as a worshiper.

Many theologians have had their say concerning this verse so I will not try to add my two cents to the deeper meanings found here. The main thing I see when I read this verse is the divine tension between truth and spirit. Both "truth" and "spirit" are necessary components of the worship experience.

When I look at this verse, I think of a flagpole with a beautiful flag flowing freely in the breeze. The flagpole is a noble thing, planted firmly in the ground, creating a firm foundation for the awaiting flag. Truth is like that. It plants us in a firm place so that when the winds of adversity blow, we remain unmoved. When I worship in truth, I am planted firmly, not directing my worship and adoration toward anything or anyone except the Lord Himself, the Father of Glory and to His Son, Jesus.

Also, truth makes a difference in the way I worship. No longer do I bring Him gifts of sacrificial animals, nor do I worship in order to receive something from Him. Truth leads me up to His throne and right before His face. It points me in the direction I need to go, and then it gives me the understanding of grace that gets me there, and finally it keeps me there.

The flag, on the other hand, instead of being fixed to one position, catches the breeze and as it does, it unfolds before all who see it. It has no capacity to move on its own. Instead, it waits for the breeze to come along and move upon it, thus allowing it to do that for which it was created.

So too, we also move when the Holy Spirit begins to move upon us. If we do not have the "spirit" aspect flowing through our worship, our own human understanding will take over and, inevitably, we will end up creating our own interpretation of what an atmosphere of worship should be like.

Jesus said, *"The wind blows wherever it pleases. You hear its sound, but you cannot tell where it comes from or where it is going. So it is with everyone born of the Spirit"* (John 3:8). We need that unpredictable, unknowable aspect of the Spirit's activity in our worship and in our lives so that He remains in control as the leader of our lives, making sure that we are dependent ones who lean upon Him and trust Him in all things.

So we see that it is the combination of flag and flagpole (spirit and truth) that allows us to truly use our liberty in a way that is firmly planted in the truth of God's nature and His Word. An empty flagpole, like truth alone, is a cold, hard object. It has been created to work with a flag, not to stand alone. So too, a flag with no flagpole, like liberty without truth, will be carried along with the breeze, forever rolling along but never held down long enough to unfurl or unveil or reveal anything to the world. Flag and flagpole. Spirit and truth. They are best when they are working together.

IT'S ALL ABOUT HIM

So here we are, coming to a close with this small offering on living a life of pure worship. As with all things good, it starts with God. "All good things come from His hands" (see James 1:17). So what is the best thing that could ever be given to a human being? More money or more power? No. More recognition or more influence? Again, it's a no.

The answer is actually pretty simple. It is *Him!* He is our exceeding great reward. He is the best thing that could ever happen to a human being. He is the best gift we will ever get.

That truth does not change when we receive Him into our hearts. We do not "move on" from God to something bigger or better. As with any type of relationship, it is not an exchange of affection if it is going one way only. And that means either way! We need to be loved and we need to love. Any relationship that moves in one direction only is doomed from the start. Yet from the start, He is waiting for us to respond to His invitation to draw near to Him.

A friend of mine once came to me to get some advice on a relationship he was involved in. After he shared some specifics, I asked him this question: "When she looks at you, do you see or feel real love and desire directed your way?"

He tilted his head and said, "Now that you mention it, no. She never gives me the feeling or the impression that she deeply cares for me. We enjoy our times together, but I don't really see any affection in her eyes."

I then suggested that this may not be the relationship that was going to be "the" one, and I prayed with him and directed him to the One who would have the right answer. He prayed about it and the relationship soon ended with everyone as friends but nothing more. Some months later he told me about a girl he had met at a wedding. As he talked, I could see a drastic difference in how he talked about her. More importantly, I could tell from the things she had told him and that I soon heard from some of her friends how much she enjoyed his company.

Soon thereafter, I met her, and for the first time I saw them together. Yes, there was "young love" going on, but I could see in her eyes a real knowledge of this man, who he was and how special he was. I saw her honor him with her words and her deeds. He came to me at that time and said, "Thank you for sharing that key question with me. With your help, I discovered that I was always giving out in relationships, and when they didn't work, I blamed myself. You made me see that it goes both ways. When my new girlfriend looks at me, I can feel love and respect coming from her. It's so very different."

And it was indeed "so very different." She's no longer just his girlfriend. Within the year, they were married and now, many years and four children later, they still look lovingly into each other's eyes as they gaze upon their beloved.

"Pure worship." What makes it pure? *Love!* Many kings have been worshiped with thousands kneeling before them. They have heard their name called out and they have seen people fall before them. But all of that has been directed one way, usually with no real affection or love connected to it at all. You can worship very easily without love. Millions have done it for years. But to worship with love—being in love and having that same love flowing back and forth between you and your God—well, that is the greatest gift of all.

The day is coming when every tongue will cry out that He is Worthy. All will see Him and all will bow—some because they have to and some because they love to. May we all bow now, not out of obligation, but out of love. And may we start enjoying an eternity of worship right here and now—restoring the lost art of pure worship.

WORTHY IS THE LAMB

(© Chris DuPré, Heart of David Music)

Worthy is the Lamb,
Son of God, Son of Man,
Worthy is the Lamb,
Who was slain on our behalf.
Every tribe and nation
Will lift up holy hands
And join with all creation—
Worthy is the Lamb.
There will be a new song
That will be heard across the land.
Every tongue will cry out—
Worthy is the Lamb.
Worthy is the Lamb
The Lamb that was slain.

ABOUT
JAMES W. GOLL

*J*ames W. Goll is the president of Encounters Network, International Director of Prayer Storm, and Founder of G.E.T. School of the Heart. He has written numerous extensive Bible study guides and is the author or coauthor of more than 25 books, including *Dream Language, The Lost Art of Intercession,* and *The Coming Israel Awakening.* James is the father of four wonderful children, resides in Franklin, Tennessee, and ministers around the world.

ABOUT
CHRIS DuPRÉ

*C*hris DuPré carries within his heart one great desire, that people would know the depths of God's great love for them. He shares with the knowledge of one who has seen God's face and knows God's heart. Originally from upstate New York, Chris spent years in Kansas City working alongside Mike Bickle to help establish the International House of Prayer. Chris recently served as associate pastor at Grace Center Church in Franklin, Tennessee. A pastor, teacher, worship leader, and spiritual father to many, Chris may best be known for his beautiful song, "Dance With Me." His new book, *The Wild Love of God*, has just been released. Chris and his wife, Laura, the parents of three lovely daughters and four beautiful grandchildren, reside in Franklin, Tennessee.

chrisdupre.com
Facebook: Chris DuPre

ABOUT
JEFF DEYO

Jeff Deyo is the founder of Worship City Ministries and the Pure Worship Institute. He is known internationally as the original lead singer of Sonicflood. He is a passionate worship leader, songwriter, speaker, actor, and author who is becoming a father figure to musicians around the globe. Jeff now holds the high honor of being a full-time faculty member ("Worship Arts Specialist, Associate Professor") at North Central University.

ABOUT
SEAN FEUCHT

Sean Feucht is a husband, father, musician, speaker, writer, revivalist, and founder of the grassroots global worship, prayer, and missions organization "Burn 24-7." His lifelong quest and dream is to witness a generation of burning hearts arise across the nations of the world with renewed faith, vision, and sacrificial pursuit after the presence of God with reckless abandonment.

ABOUT
JULIE MEYER

*J*ulie Meyer is a longtime and beloved worship leader and songwriter at the International House of Prayer in Kansas City. She is a prophetic singer who carries the glory and the presence of God as an abandoned worshipper. Her passion is His presence as she trumpets the message of the Bridegroom searching for His Bride!

She is the author of *Invitation to Encounter*, a recording artist with several CDs. She has traveled the world, leading worship and speaking on the hearing the voice of God, sharing her encounters with the Lord, and encouraging the Body of Christ to dream.

www.juliemeyer.com

ABOUT
RACHEL GOLL TUCKER

Rachel Goll Tucker is a singer/songwriter from Nashville, Tennessee. She is the lead singer and songwriter along with her husband in their band, August York. Rachel studied songwriting at Belmont University and acting at the New York Conservatory for Dramatic Arts. You may contact Rachel by email at: rachelrtucker@gmail.com or by website at: www.augustyork.com

IN THE RIGHT HANDS, THIS BOOK WILL CHANGE LIVES!

Most of the people who need this message will not be looking for this book. To change their lives, you need to put a copy of this book in their hands.

> *But others (seeds) fell into good ground, and brought forth fruit, some a hundred-fold, some sixty-fold, some thirty-fold* (Matthew 13:8).

Our ministry is constantly seeking methods to find the good ground, the people who need this anointed message to change their lives. Will you help us reach these people?

> *Remember this—a farmer who plants only a few seeds will get a small crop. But the one who plants generously will get a generous crop* (2 Corinthians 9:6).

EXTEND THIS MINISTRY BY SOWING
3 BOOKS, 5 BOOKS, 10 BOOKS, OR MORE TODAY,
AND BECOME A LIFE CHANGER!

Thank you,

Don Nori Sr., Founder
Destiny Image
Since 1982

DESTINY IMAGE PUBLISHERS, INC.

"Promoting Inspired Lives."

VISIT OUR NEW SITE HOME AT
WWW.DESTINYIMAGE.COM

FREE SUBSCRIPTION TO DI NEWSLETTER

Receive free unpublished articles by top DI authors, exclusive
discounts, and free downloads from our best and newest books.

Visit www.destinyimage.com to subscribe.

Write to:	Destiny Image
	P.O. Box 310
	Shippensburg, PA 17257-0310
Call:	1-800-722-6774
Email:	orders@destinyimage.com

For a complete list of our titles or to place an order
online, visit www.destinyimage.com.